"The title of Patti White's *Particularly Dangerous Situation* may refer to a storm, perhaps even an apocalyptic one. It might refer to some collective delusion, or it might refer to the situation of living in a world that can produce such a storm. In the end, however, White's dangerous situation comes down to the intellectual and artistic risk this lyrically narrative collection makes: turning disaster into art. White—who lived through a tornado that devastated Tuscaloosa, Alabama, in 2011—has a survivor's sense of devastation tempered by an artist's desire to transform the world. With a poet's sense of language and gifted storyteller's pacing, White channels voices (like Faulkner in *As I Lay Dying*) which provide lenses for understanding a loss that each one struggles to conceive, but the struggle to tell their stories on their terms provides the terra firma of this unique novella. After all, as White writes, '[We] are caught in a narrative that might not be survivable.'"

~ Jeff Newberry, co-author of *Cross Country*

"Poet Patti White concocts with this stunning and stuttering prose engine, *Particularly Dangerous Situation*, a Medusa-haired memo war on the fly, a transcript of Traumatic Stress Disorder before it gets a chance to be Post. I kept thinking of what black and white disasters were befalling Kansas when Toto wasn't there anymore. White's draining novella is all Coriolis effect and falling isobars of emotion, rich in vortices and bowing echoes of booming syntax. Diaphanous and occluded, the book is a catalogue of jagged and jittery clouds—mackerel smacked, nightmare's tails, an Old Testament hardware store of hammers and anvils."

~ Michael Martone, author of *The Moon Over Wapakoneta* and *Brooding*

"*Particularly Dangerous Situation* consumes and entrances. In fact I became Jonah in the belly of a twister built by White. Each page—each sentence—is another edge, ledge, ledger, conflagration. And yet for every collapsing absence in this tour-de-force, White's poet-steeped prose wills a luminous architecture by which to know the way. And just as I finished this scorcher, I began it again. There is no finer compliment than that arc traced by leaping back to word one. This is White at her finest. I urge you toward *PDS* today!"

~ Abraham Smith, author of *Destruction of Man*

Patti White

# Particularly Dangerous Situation

A NOVELLA

Arc Pair Press
Tacoma, WA

ISBN-13: 978-1-7339719-3-5

Library of Congress Control Number: 2019952518

Cover design by Brian Oliu
Spanish translations by Victoria Jeanne Martinez

*for Tuscaloosa*

# ONE

# Weatherman

When I tell you it is a Particularly Dangerous Situation, that means you should prepare for a disaster in your town today. That the dew point is high, the atmosphere soupy, the rotation factors off the charts. That soon the sky will lower and swarm and spin and you will be unable to stand in the face of it. Buildings will disappear. Water will be contaminated. The social order will collapse. So when I say hunker down, you must go to your safe place and pull a big thick blanket over your head.

When I tell you it is a Particularly Dangerous Situation, I do so with all the authority of the National Weather Service behind me. Let me show you this white area on the map. That is your town and the town next to it and a few counties more, and all of it, every elementary school and church of it, rests in a swale of humid air that is moving. And that air carries things you cannot imagine, the dust of Africa, the last traces of Mt. St. Helens, the heat from rooftops in Atlanta, the sweat of racehorses, the evaporation of your backyard swimming pool. It is already laden but it can carry so much more.

Do you have a helmet in your safe place? If not you can put a cooking pot over your head. Do you have bottles of water, a noisemaker, a crowbar, a power bar, your medications? Maybe you should write your name on your arm with a Sharpie. Maybe you should be wearing jeans and work boots. Maybe you should have a gun. Some people think holy water will help. Do you have a chainsaw? Have you thought about where you will go if the world as you know it comes to an end? Do you remember the bodies falling from the Twin Towers, the clouds of dust, the sudden darkness? Maybe it will be something like that. It is a Particularly Dangerous Situation.

Some of you are already ignoring me. Look, you say, the sun is out. The clouds are white and fluffy, a stiff breeze blowing, a damp breeze blowing, but the sun is out and I have to take the kids to the park. And you will get in your SUV and stop for a bag of tacos and the trees make it impossible to see the horizon so you won't see what's coming. You will wait until you see it overhead and then it will be too late. Your kids will be sucked out of the car and disappear. You will live your whole life regretting that simple decision, the park and the tacos, though in fact your life will be remarkably short, because a dangerous situation does not end with the first deaths. No it does not.

# Carleen Hicks

I like the way sheets smell after drying on the line, but in the South you don't get much laundry weather, the air always so humid, so full of pollen and bugs. My mama had a clothes pole like a blown-out umbrella. I remember her spinning it around to reach the next section of line, hanging up papa's shirts, draping the bath towels, making little rosebuds of undies and socks. I remember the pillowcases snapping in the wind. And that's what my mind turns to when I think about that day, the spinning of the umbrella, the white linens like shrouds, a cuff or a collar caught on a wooden pin. The wind turning the pole and spiraling things up into the sky. And afterward the trees like clotheslines, hung with dresses and insulation, quilts and wallpaper. All tatters and shreds. Broken skeleton trees, oaks and pines, magnolias draped with something I couldn't quite see. Something flapping in the leftover wind. It had a kind of glassy sheen. I didn't know how to call it at the time.

I do know that I listened to the weatherman that morning and called my daughter over to Mississippi to see if they had storms already, but she never answered. I kept an eye on the sky all day and by afternoon I could see the clouds curdle up and turn yellow and the rain crows were in the crape myrtles. I called my daughter again but still no answer and now the weatherman looked scared. The radar map behind him was spackled hot pink inside the reds and oranges and he was talking numbers and somewhere on the road the storm chaser was lost among the pines, a road with no signs whatsoever and his video signal was weak. I was opening the windows in my house when the weatherman said to take shelter, so I went into the bathroom with a couch cushion over my head, but you know an old dogtrot house is a misery in weather. That flimsy it just wants to fall over on itself.

I left the tv turned up loud but the power went and I could smell the electric sizzle in the walls. And oh the howling. The wind got up under the front porch and inside the rafters, boards ripping and popping and then the barbeque grill hit the siding and scraped and rattled and now glass and maybe some bones breaking and I was praying out loud and seeing stars. Then it was over and quiet like the grave except the rain was coming through the ceiling. Water spattering on the floor and the light so green with leaves and not a word from the tv no more. I felt so blessed coming out of that bathroom, so lucky to be alive. But you and I know that isn't really true, don't we? We know that it is just as dangerous and awful to be alive as to be dead. Maybe more so.

# Colonel Stanton

The satellites saw it right away. Not just a blankness under the cloud cover but a slickness to the screen that made your skin crawl. Something uncanny in how the land looked or didn't. The roads all sideways and the lines blurred. Or towns off the grid and falling dark. And when you think about a blackout in the south, you think hurricanes. Swamps rising over the roads, the mangroves heavy with mosquitoes and snakes. You think terrible infections and food spoiling and the cockroaches flying. Like after Katrina. Water over the levees in New Orleans, and up in Mississippi the pines snapped off like toothpicks. No AC for weeks and people getting crazy with heat. So maybe like that, except maybe not.

When we saw what we saw on the screen we started moving resources out of Alabama. Search crews for rescue and recovery, MREs and generators, truckloads of water. Troops for security. Medical supplies. A small convoy of men and matériel. And when we drove to Mississippi, we ended up in Louisiana. The trucks went on through like Mississippi wasn't there. And when we turned back, there was nothing between us and Alabama. Just emptiness and rising mists and not a soul to be found. Piles of rubble here and there and a few armadillos we flattened on the way through the first time. Maybe a crumpled water tower and a broken tree with insulation flapping or windshield wipers and a long bridge.

I don't have any words for what happened there. But in my mind Mississippi still exists, the devil's crossroad and the hot tamale trail, the blues oozing out of the mud, Billy Joe's bridge, the cannons at Vicksburg and the pink azaleas, the catfish and pulled pork and all those cotton fields. And I can hear the cowbells at the state college as the football game heats up. I just can’t see them. No one can see them.

## Juan Reyes

Those tamales in Mississippi? Those are cooked by black folks in the delta. From when *mexicanos* worked the fields side by side. If you want tamales you come to my house. The meat seasoned with peppers grown *bajo el cielo de Nuestra Señora*, such a blue sky and no clouds. The people say Hatch, but the best chiles come from my cousins in Chimayo. You know the high road to Taos? coming down, Chamisal, Las Trampas, Truchas, then Chimayo where the peppers grow in hidden fields, very secret, and the Santuario has a tree full of rosaries and a well of holy dirt. People come to be healed and they throw their crutches away. It is a town of much devotion, much faith. *Muy escondido, muy sagrado*.

So that day I was at the *carnicería* and when I came out it was a bowl of *masa* rising thick and hot. It was a *poblano* swollen and charred. That is what it looked like to me. The sky all the wrong colors. It made me sick and I fell on my knees in the parking lot. My legs gave out from me and I collapsed under that horrible sky. I felt the gravel on my palms, very hard and sharp. Across the street the paint store exploded and the power lines snapped and whipped and sparked and everything was coming apart. I crawled through rattlesnakes. The traffic signals dropped like vultures and I was crazy with the fear that was shining on my skin and hanging from the broken light poles.

You ask me what a Nissan sounds like when it falls from the sky? Have you seen a train run off the tracks? An oak tree passing overhead sounds like the unwinding of a clock. I heard a swarm of locusts. I heard a volcano cracking open. I don't know what they were in real life. I was on my knees and then crawling and the air so full of things. The air howling with skulls that still have flesh. And I heard the *grito del tiempo*, the screaming of time as it leaves the world. I had gravel stuck in my palms and my knees and my ears were bleeding. The sky green and yellow and like charcoal burning and then my head blank like a tv screen after the remote.

# Vesuvia Morris

For a while it rained bodies.

# Lila Jane Smith

I am at the dentist. On the chair-side tv a video of a chimpanzee brushing its teeth, creepy monkey grin all minty fresh, a bird feeder outside the picture window, little chickadees or whatever. The sound of drills making me nervous. Then I'm watching black clouds over the river, Armageddon clouds, black with green sparks like alien lights. You talk about a tornado funnel but this is just a solid mass of darkness moving real slow, real serious and deliberate. Sirens going off all over town, the birds panicked, the hygienist screaming about her mother. I see transformers sparking, a fire truck falling in the water, strange plastic people floating down, Lego firemen or Barbie dolls. Everyone at the dentist is already gone. I'm strapped to the chair like a serial killer, like someone desperate for a pencil sharpener, the clouds so thick I can't see and then the window breaks.

When I come to it's a blank computer screen with no graphics. A cursor blinking somewhere and no sound. I look up and see blue sky. The chair is perfectly still inside the eye of the tornado. I am suffocated in the cone of silence. My eyes are bleeding. I can't see where the river is now and all I can think of is the flying monkeys. I don't know how I am going to get home. I am sitting in a dentist's chair crying tears of blood and things are spinning around me, dogs and crates of petunias, pine straw and hammers, all the small things. Maybe some diamonds. Maybe someone's silver tea set. Things shining in the wall of cloud.

I don't know how long I wait for it to move. Just holding onto the arms of the chair. Waiting to be taken up like the rapture. Holding on and then it's all black and shiny and so loud my brain explodes.

# Everett Davis

I know the houses in this town. I have a map in my head all the time. The good neighborhoods and school districts. Where the firehouses are. Traffic flow and food deserts. Interest rates. So I think of myself as an informed person of the city. I know the history of the cactus house, the Stringtown Motel, the unmarked slave cemetery. I take people to eat cornbread and butterbeans at Missy's. I show them how the river turns back on itself beyond the fall line, the last rib of Appalachian shale before the land heads down to the gulf. I know the bones of this country like my own.

On that day I met clients in a vacant house. A RELO from Indiana. They walked around looking for dead cockroaches and stained ceilings. They used all the code words to talk about pocket neighborhoods close to downtown. They asked about crime watch and association dues and no soliciting. They measured the rooms. One of them asked about a video in the hotel breakfast room. I hadn't seen the forecast but the day was humid and heavy. It felt like weather. The couple looked unsettled by the low pressure. And they were cranky with hunger and rising wind and the idea of all that packing ahead.

I went out on the front porch to check the sky. The overgrown camellias under the pines made the yard look like a fish bowl. The porch swing had leprosy, peeled white paint and gnawed-up edges. I could hear the woman in the kitchen saying "bubble wrap! bubble wrap!" and there was a wind chime going crazy and the air felt like warm wet towels, too thick to breathe. The radar app on my phone showed red and orange and hot pink. Back inside the couple was fussing about the fireplace. They didn't like the closets. They wanted to see more houses. Think about that. They wanted to see more houses.

Then I could hear it. The sound of hell moving. The walls vibrated. Like in the movies. You know it's either an earthquake or a tornado or the T-Rex is coming. The sirens from the university clock tower went off. The man was shouting about stairs, but the south has no basements. So we squeezed into the cedar closet in the central hallway. Like Vienna sausages. Like bodies in a coffin. Then the house broke apart and maybe some of us were dead. Or not. I'm still not sure. But I know those Indiana people aren't out looking at houses. There aren't any houses around here.

## Tallulah Ballou

A book is a bastion. A labyrinth. A far country with maps you can't quite follow. A good book has gargoyles on the cathedral, broken rose windows, opium incense. It makes the world stranger and more intense. So I keep a book with me always. On the day of the storm, it was a first edition of *The Great Gatsby*. You know that dust jacket, the enormous eyes, the neon skyline, a haunted night in blue? So revealing, golden bodies in the irises, the green streak of a tear halfway down the cheek, electric wires strung from side to side. Designed by Francis Cugat even before the manuscript was completed, all the desire and sorrow and entrapment laid out in gouache. I don't know how many times I've read that book. Maybe six times. Maybe twenty.

I was in my car, heading uphill from the library to downtown and I know I wasn't respecting the polygon. I was thinking about the molar cufflinks and the valley of ashes. I stopped at the light at the top of the hill and suddenly it was behind me. In my rearview mirror. A wall of spinning trees, road signs, flashes of insulation, what looked like a million books dropping like blocks of ice. Monstrous in every sense of the word and dazzling, literally mesmerizing. I stared without breathing. I could feel the car pull backward as if the funnel was magnetized and I was thinking gravity, that the weight of my old Impala would hold me in place. There was a red SUV further down the hill and I saw three people sucked up out of the windows, I actually saw them take flight and disappear into the cloud. Then I ran the light and drove and drove all the way to the state line before I turned around.

The thing about books is you can put them down. Come back later. What I keep thinking about the tornado is that there's no stopping it, nothing that turns it aside, no way to mitigate or negotiate the effects. That it was so relentless, so deliberate. As if it were motivated. As if it had a map and a list. As if it were a plot untwisting itself across the landscape and all the characters were already dead and didn't know it. Like that movie. Or like we all are, I guess. We who are in life are already in death. Everything in literature and philosophy tells us so. We only have to pay attention. We only have to look at the forecast to know what's coming.

# TWO

# Weatherman

When I say this is a generational weather event I mean that no one living will see this happen again. Decades will pass without a hint of weather. Forecasters will go mad with boredom. Of course it will rain. The wind will get up in winter. Cirrus clouds will feather the sky. But this storm will be the last such storm we will see. The wide black funnels with octopus arms. The critical paths of death. The scouring of the earth. If you are living now, you will not see this again.

When I say this is a generational weather event, I do so in the course of long-form weather reporting, standing in front of a camera with the radar projected on a screen behind me. I have been on camera for hours and there are hours yet to go. My white shirt makes a nice contrast against the reds and pinks on the screen. I want to show you the live feed from the storm chasers but we have lost the signal. The last shot we had was of a car tunneling through hail and pine trees whipping across the road. The last shot we had was of a church spire collapsing. The last shot we had was of a town square so darkened by clouds that the lights had come on. And gone off again. And the town was there but dark or not there. We couldn't tell.

Maybe you have researched the generations in your family tree. You know who died at Chickamauga. Which ancestor came from Ireland or had Spanish flu or built bridges during the Great Depression. Who you were named after and who the family tried to hide but the records were still there waiting to be discovered. And this will be like that, a tale to be told to the ones who live after, who have never seen such destruction, who think of us as ghosts wandering through the pines. The generations to come will speak of us with wonder and dread. It is that kind of event.

# Vesuvia Morris

For a while it rained bodies. I heard them fall like horrible hail, thunk thunk thunk out in the parking lot. Some set off car alarms. Some fell right in front of the windows. We heard them land on the roof, thunk thunk, louder than you'd think. Not like an axe breaking a skull, that watermelon sound, but more like concrete blocks hitting earth. Like Godzilla stomping a Japanese village. Like my father falling on the porch, his thick body on the planks. Solid against solid. And so loud.

I was in the craft store looking for watercolors. Mine were painted out and I wanted a new set and some brushes. When the sirens went off we huddled against the walls and some people covered their heads with Indian throws or embroidered cushions, but I looked out. And I saw them like it was a terrorist day but no one was on fire. Just wet and shiny like mannequins, all arms and legs and silent but for the landing. Too many to count. A rain of some kind of humanity but I wouldn't like to say what kind. They didn't seem local to me. I'm not sure what I mean by that.

My father said I was too tall for a woman, too angular and dark. I have his long bones and his hands, but he was a square man. So when he fell it was like an oak tree in a storm. In my mind he split the porch rail and impaled himself on the pickets, but in fact he fell flat and his heart spilled out of his mouth. The planks too solid to give. His body too wide and heavy. No one tried to pick him up until the ambulance. We just left him on the porch and went back in to finish breakfast. It was biscuits and gravy and so good.

# Juan Reyes

I walked all the way home. Holding my arms out with my palms bleeding like Jesus, *Sangre de Cristo*, *la sangre de la misericordia*, the stigmata on my hands. The power lines in front of me. The fallen trees and crushed cars and body parts scattered on the road. I climbed over the dead and the living. I crawled and sobbed and knelt on the pavement and no one saw me. Part of me was in Chamisal watching the rabbit brush turn into gold, the waters of the creek running clear, my head was in hallucinations, and when I looked again the sky was bitter white and a dead cat was in my arms.

I walked home past houses on top of houses. I tried to pick the gravel out of my skin and found shards of glass. My arm glinted in the light. My skin gleamed with sweat or sorrow or maybe the sap of the broken trees. I walked home on pavement that was missing, the asphalt torn away. I know I walked through screams as thick as butter. I know the dead cat opened its eyes and blinked. What did it see, I asked myself. I went into a church maybe Baptist, forgive me, it was so dim inside the adobe walls of San José de Gracia, so thick and cool those walls, the candles always burning, maybe I was not right in the head. I prayed for all the souls. I slept for a minute on a pew, blood clotted on my palms, my clothes in tatters. No one saw me. No one saw me sleeping in the church.

I walked all the way home on streets I've never seen before. Front yards full of pink insulation and hubcaps. Stripped pines bent double. Chicken wire wrapped around mailboxes. I passed people in blankets stumbling over bricks. I saw a child with a chainsaw. I walked with my eyes full of tears. I saw two men playing *fútbol* with a red ball or a bloody head my eyes full of tears from the grit of the wind that still howled inside my mind. I carried the cat all the way, its fur cold and stiff. I walked and no one saw me and when I got home I wasn't alive.

## Carleen Hicks

My arm was broken but it didn't matter. I made a sling out of an old shirt and sat out on the front porch waiting for rescue. The house was smothered by branches that stuck through windows and poked down from the rafters. One limb had a piece of Easter grass twisted around the end and it put me in mind of baked ham and scalloped potatoes and how hungry I was waiting for someone to tell me where to go. Dogs barked all over like they do when boys joyride through and take baseball bats to the mailboxes. I thought I could hear sirens in the center of town. I waited a long time and I could hear gunshots and screams and there were fires on the horizon. Or maybe that was a show I saw one time and it got in my head. Maybe it was a leafy green afternoon and dead quiet, the trees cradling the property and all the dogs asleep. Maybe it wasn't smoke but dusk falling. The house creaking behind me and the shadows thickening like gravy. The screech of a wrought-iron gate.

My momma always said I had a high tolerance for pain. That time my cousin dropped the blade edge of an oar on the crown of my head and I saw stars for an hour. Or when my daddy cut me instead of the pig he meant to butcher, his knife-hand slick with blood and my leg somehow in the way. I never cried out, neither time. So I took my broken arm inside and gathered up my things, made a budget out of a pillow case and got my hairbrush and study Bible and a photo of my daughter Susie. The sunlight in that picture falling on her Easter bonnet like a blessing from God. The basket over her arm, full of eggs and candy. Her daddy is taking the picture and you can see his shadow on the ground stretching toward her like the tower of doom. Little Susie in the sunlight.

So I sat with my budget and my pain on a porch that was half gone and listened to the tail end of the wind. I could smell rain still falling somewhere close and things were slicking through the bushes as the light went. Of course the electric was out so it was the darkest night in the world and I was hungry. Wishing for banana pudding. I thought about all the times I'd been broken and carried on. I thought about the war that killed Susie's daddy and how glad I was that he never came home. I prayed about that some. I prayed about my Susie in Mississippi and how that football team always has cowbells ringing. It was dawn before I saw another person who was alive.

# Everett Davis

Aftermath. The mathematics of the after time. How you count up the dead and the missing. The number of damaged homes, how much roadway will need to be resurfaced, how long the power will be out. Think about wind speed, the width and length of the debris field. How insurance payouts are calculated. Think about police tape and barricades. And that FEMA cross: a quadrant for the unit making the search, one for the date, one for hazards in the property, one for the number of dead or living found. Didn't that just pop into your head, the spray paint in bright colors? The graffiti of catastrophe on every building or pile of rubble. Myself, I counted two missing but I didn't have any paint; just insect repellent in the car trunk along with my placards and posts: FOR SALE and OPEN HOUSE.

I searched the property as best I could without gloves and a crowbar. Called their names. Listened for moans and whimpers. Thought about how fragile a house really is, the guts spilled out of this one, shreds of insulation, splintered wood and broken glass, wires and pipes exposed, everything smaller and more delicate than you believed when you were safe inside. Like how you think a body is strong until you see how easily it turns liquid under a baseball bat. So much of the body is ocean. I read that somewhere. So anyway I looked for bodies living or dead. I called and called and then just walked away. Thinking Indiana people, probably self-reliant and resilient and used to storms of various proportions, including blizzards but almost certainly tornadoes as well.

I didn't have a scratch on me. Count me lucky. The windows were broken out of my car but the engine turned over like Joe Isuzu. Then I saw the roads were blocked with fallen oaks and power lines and I was trapped where I was unless I wanted to crawl over tree trunks in my suit. Which I did, finally. Because it was clear the first responders would be a while. The sirens were all going somewhere else. The CDC says be prepared for up to a week before help arrives. It says to shelter in place. But this wasn't a place anymore. It was a cross on a piece of plywood. It was something for the cadaver dogs to investigate. It was where Indiana became a figment of someone's imagination or a last memory or the name of a stranger who disappeared when you weren't looking.

# Tallulah Ballou

When I got back to town the roads were blocked by police and ambulances. Bodies were being carried out on doors. In wheelbarrows. In the beds of pickup trucks. I saw strips of Mylar hanging from a light post, a television clinging to a tree. A rosary draped over a fire hydrant. I walked through a maze of unrecognizable buildings, completely lost in my own neighborhood. The streets were full of flashing lights and rainwater and souls who had survived, hundreds of people who had crawled out of basements and meat lockers. People who had shifted refrigerators and bookcases and mattresses. Now they stood in their yards and driveways in wonder and shock. Or they moved slowly and steadily. Off balance. Like zombies shambling toward the living. With blood running down their faces, silent and stark raving mad. Like Ishmael after the whale. Staring into or out of the abyss.

I saw people taking selfies with the dead. Posing in front of the ruins of the taco place with that enormous neon cactus fallen and shattered. I saw legs with no body. And a mannequin naked and wet with rain. I walked and walked. Tripped over wires and bits of metal. Looked sideways at things huddled under the azaleas. I walked slowly like the wounded, my movements jerky and odd, as if my joints were bewildered. Finally I sat on a curb and put my head in my hands. I closed my eyes and listened and then I heard the cries and wails and the chainsaws. I heard more sirens and a screech like the wheels of a train running off the tracks. I felt people pass me without speaking. The footsteps of the living dead. That's what I thought then. That the storm had created a whole population of living dead. I had no idea at the time. Just no idea.

Nietzsche said that when you gaze into the abyss, the abyss also gazes into you. That when you fight monsters you risk becoming the monster. So you see the monster bearing down and you take shelter. The sound of the storm breaks your veins open or a wall of books collapses on you or maybe those were bricks. You come out of the basement with your eyes unable to blink. Walk down the street holding your broken arms. Carrying children who will never speak again. Or you sit on the slab of what was once a house, clutching a frenzied dog that bites you and runs away. The dead are all around you and maybe everyone is dead just a little bit or a lot. So you take a butcher knife and cut your own throat. Or you sit beside a stranger on the curb just quietly seeing the end of life as you've known it.

## Lila Jane Smith

I am a flying monkey screeching through the clouds.

# Colonel Stanton

We took the resources back to Alabama to clean up after the storm there. All the tents and MREs and mobile communications and medical supplies. All the generators and heavy equipment. But in the South people are resilient and prepared. Local folks had already broken out the chain saws and started clearing trees off the roads. Churches handed out sandwiches. Kids dragged red wagons full of bottled water. ROTC cadets tarped roofs. Teenagers brought garbage bags to clear out refrigerators and litter boxes. The local paper had already started a list of the missing and dead.

My troops were on orders not to talk about Mississippi. Not to say what we had seen or not seen there. We identified a perimeter and set checkpoints to funnel legitimate property owners into safe areas. The mayor was doing photo ops at the hospital and the football stadium and the fire station, and I heard the President might helicopter in for a walk-through. Power crews were dispatched from Michigan and Kentucky. Someone trucked in a load of ice. Journalists showed up with satellite connections and bright lights. It was a scene I was familiar with, the same thing you've seen on television a dozen times or more.

Then a call came in about the mannequins. Someone had stacked a bunch of mannequins in the parking lot at the mall and someone else claimed to have seen one move. Said it got up and walked away. When a patrol car got there, there were no mannequins, nobody in the parking lot, just SUVs with broken windows. Then more calls. Invisible people with invisible blood. Shiny things coming out of the bushes. Something flapping in the wind. Someone claimed children were luring women into the rubble to be gang-raped. Someone else had seen a satanic ritual. Or serial killers wrapping bodies in tin foil. Our own men were sending back reports: The wounded were cutting their own throats. The wounded were screaming. The wounded had lost their souls.

When rumors go viral in a population they collide and reshape themselves. Soon we were hearing about mannequins raping children. About invisible murders and airborne knives buzzing overhead like drones. About a colony of disembodied souls huddled in the undergrowth. We heard the President's helicopter had crashed and burned. We heard about children flapping their wings like mutant crows rising out of a corn field. Flying away into the sunset. We did find a couple of bodies with gunshot wounds to the head. And an arm hacked off at the shoulder. So some bad things were happening true enough. Normal bad things. Looters and arsonists and scam artists, people who feed on disaster and make it worse. But no werewolves or demons or whatever.

# THREE

# Weatherman

When I say that it is best to be two-dimensional during a storm, I mean that pieces of paper travel well in the wind. A tornado can carry a photograph 200 miles and set it down without a crumple or tear or even a hint of dampness. So if you cannot hunker down in a safe place you must become as paper. Think of flatness. Extend your arms and press your body to the ground. Then if the tornado takes you, it will bear you up in tendrils of cloud, in long white fingers of condensation. The storm will let you drift and waft and settle like a leaf on a field of cotton. Or on a patch of concrete. In either case, it is better to be light and flat, to be paper, to carry an image of something long past and fading.

When I say that a tornado can carry paper a great distance, I mean that cattle will be transported to another pasture and skinned alive or dead by whirling gravel. That rocking chairs will appear on alien porches and pickets from a wrought-iron fence will arrow into a bed of bearded iris. A crystal teardrop from a chandelier, a boxed set of state quarters, an empty suitcase, a teacup and saucer, these will be caught in a divergent current until dispersed by the collapsing supercell. When I say a tornado can carry paper I mean the updraft will lift trucks high above the ground and crash them down on your head. Trees will be plucked up out of the earth and replanted elsewhere. And no one will know where anything came from. Except for the cancelled checks and receipts and you will see those on television, along with the child's shoe and the skeleton of a cat.

When I speak of these things perhaps you will think of the Biblical rain of frogs. Or the rain of blood that soaked Richard the Lionheart. I tell you these signs and wonders are in fact so commonplace they appear in meteorology textbooks. Frogs get sucked up as a waterspout passes over the pond. Rain becomes infused with Saharan dust or the soot from coal fires or the spores of microalgae. Trentepholia in the Inter-Tropical Convergence Zone. Iron oxide from dried swamps. The small detritus of the world borne aloft and mixed with the humid air of the Deep South. This is what you will see: A red rain staining your clothes. The frogs sliding off your skin and hopping away.

No one ever forecasts displacements or discolorations. But what I want to tell you is that whatever falls from the sky was once a part of the earth. That some things will fall more slowly or in places more unexpected than others. And that it is well to be two-dimensional in a storm. Think of flatness. Be the paper.

# Juan Reyes

My house was empty. I put the cat on the mantel and went from room to room, all the furniture gone, the rugs sucked up off the floors, only Our Lady of Guadalupe, the holy water font from the Ave María Grotto, all the miniature buildings there so careful and to scale, the gift shop full of *milagros*, and this was one too, the little cup of *agua bendita* by the door. My wife she was not there and my children and I shouted at the walls as if they could answer. The cat was silent from the fireplace but my voice echoed like the house on moving day, freshly painted by my own crew and the truck and boxes waiting on the street, *mi tía* Esperanza placing a pot of cilantro on the kitchen counter. My voice came back to me in tones of dread and I knew that this was no longer my life, a yard full of children and tomato plants, a workday full of ladders and tarps, a pail of brushes waiting to be cleaned. I knew that the cat was dead or alive and that my house was empty.

I had nothing but the clothes on my back and I slept on the wooden floor I was so tired and vacant in my head. I washed my bloody hands in the sink and folded them over my chest like a dead man and dreamed of lava fields, the *Jornada del Muerto*, the lava crusted and hard. But the dawn was green leaves over the windows and the cat curled against my stomach like a cool brick of plaster and I didn't know if I had put it there or it had moved in the night. I refused to name it, I did not want to own the cat, but I would have called it Roswell, so uncanny and alien, the almond eyes almost closed or open. When I was a boy we drove the highway of abductions, ate *huevos rancheros* at the cantina, waited for darkness, watched the skies for the hanging lights, the falling saucers promised in every brochure. But there was nothing. Only the stars, the dust on the highway. The way headlights appeared in the distance.

In the backyard I found a piece of paper, an invoice from a lumberyard in Yazoo City, split rails for a long fence, *una hacienda* that one, a big order from a month ago. I folded it and put it in my back pocket. Someone in Mississippi would want that one day, I thought. They would frame it and put it in the shop, sit with their coffee and smoke, talk about how far their invoice had traveled on the day of the terrible storm. Also I found an umbrella, tightly wound, twisted and snapped shut. It belonged to no one in my house, such a black and unhappy thing. But *mis hijos*, no. The swing set gone. The toy trucks and sand shovels. Nothing in the yard to say I had ever been a father, and even the grass, so flat and yellow, the life sucked out of it by the wind.

I thought then about the Red Cross and FEMA and maybe *mi familia* in a shelter somewhere, blankets around their shoulders and sipping hot drinks, on the table a jigsaw puzzle of Venice, reflections in the canal, the buildings with their feet in water, such rich colors, ochre and magenta, cerulean, the little pieces forming a picture the children will never forget. I picked up the cat and walked away from my house forever. I wanted to look for my wife among the living or the dead, to see my sons fighting over an orange or a pillow or sitting quietly with a book on the bleachers, the high ceiling of a gymnasium swallowing their breath, in and out, their small chests rising, then falling. I wanted to see their bodies warm with sleep. I wanted a hot meal. I wanted those tamales with the Chimayo peppers. I walked out of the house with a dead cat, forgive me, I could not leave it behind.

## Vesuvia Morris

I never did get those watercolors. Half the roof caved in and brought a cascade of bodies with it. Broken beams and sheets of plywood and tarpaper, wire frames for the hanging ceiling, light fixtures, all mixed up with legs and arms and torsos. A cubist collapse, everything at right angles to itself. It's something I might want to paint someday and I think it will be like *Guernica* without the horses. A painting that screams and cuts you but with throw pillows and artificial flowers everywhere, the shoppers huddled against the wall and then crawling toward daylight or rainlight to some space that isn't full of terrible things no crafter should ever see.

Outside the sky was still green with hail over the north end of town. Cars were crushed and tumbled in the lot and broken glass covered the asphalt. Shards or diamonds and chrome buggies and the remnants of sale signs and flags. Men from the computer repair shop were already stacking the fallen bodies, which had stiffened into jigsaw puzzles or Pick-up Sticks, fitting together in odd ways that looked intentional. Like an art installation or a very complex statue on the theme of holocaust. Those black and white movies of the liberation of the camps. The skeletal survivors. Bulldozers shoving the dead into mass graves. The film crackling in the projector and dust making lightning on the screen. Or after the tsunami, that photo of the driftwood that was really the dead washed up on shore. Bodies as an art form.

People wandered dazed and bleeding out of modernist doorways. My skirt flapped in the wind and it was torn and maybe my hair was on fire or that was smoke blowing sideways from downtown. I stood still, waiting for sirens, but the storm bodies gleamed and beckoned so I walked over and touched one.

My hand came away startled. The skin was cool as plastic, dry as a hen's egg, but there was a tremor, a thrumming under my palm. It seemed like the arm I touched might swell up and explode, or maybe the body would unfold itself and move. I didn't linger. Instead, I turned toward the rubble of the mall and when I looked back the computer geeks had disappeared.

The women from the craft store were trying to go back inside. Searching for someone who might or might not be dead. I waited on the sidewalk, hearing their cries of discovery or dismay, listening for a waterfall of roof tiles, thinking about where inside the art supplies had been located. Back home—if there was a home still standing—I had a painting in progress on the easel. This one in oil, a study of a house smothered in kudzu. I could see now that painting was all wrong. It had no edges. It didn't account for the chaos Picasso saw wherever he looked. The horses screaming. The polygons and cubes and angles just under the skin of life. That painting had no storm, and I would have to paint over it when I got home.

# Lila Jane Smith

I am a flying monkey screeching through the clouds. I hear bells clang like a metal drum breaking my ears. I see petunias in bloom. A neon sign buzzing acid green. I am moving through air so thick and wet I can hardly breathe. Like when Gary Sinise goes to Mars in that awful movie. The sandstorm and then that alien ship takes him away in a vat of liquid air. But I have to say I don't understand gravity. The Lego men fell into the river and the Barbie dolls fell but it's like the earth doesn't matter now. I think if I look down I might see my house. Or Kansas. But everything passes beneath me like a GPS satellite that's blanked out on the screen.

Sometimes things hit me and I look at my skin for bruises but what I see is shine. I feel polished like the sugar scrub at the spa. Scraped clean and left smooth. Flakes and scales swept up or washed down a drain and my heart has stopped but a terrible sound vibrates in my bones. I don't know how to say what my body feels and I wonder if the dentist's chair will fall apart soon. How much can something made in China take? Piece of junk faux-leather industrial design. But I hold tight to the arms in this bright darkness. In which petunias are pink fire. Or purple and white streak lightning. Flashes that make no shadows.

The cloud is full of people who shine. I see them flailing through a rainy patch, pale arms and legs, hair streaming wet. Maybe they are swimming through the storm but it looks a lot like drowning to me. Hands reaching for a surface. Mouths open like goldfish, darker bodies more like sharks moving in. More like an oil slick on the waves. Then they are gone and there are fences at the far edges and a bloated cow with its legs turned up. How long before something dead swells up like that? Maybe it was already dead and floated up like a balloon. I check my arm to see if it's swollen but it looks like plastic wrap pulled straight out of the box. Tight and shining. Self-contained and deliberate.

I think there are houses here and if I dared to leave the chair I could crawl into one and find shelter from the wind. Find a quiet corner and sleep like a head injury and wake up to see someone walking down the highway. White lines guiding them. I think houses, maybe a cattle farm with sheds, and I know there are trees with giant root systems. I know there are cars with children gazing out the windows. I want to wave at them but what if I let go and the chair falls away and I drift like in space? No gravity up here, just an endless universe inside the clouds and petunias and monkeys and the people who swim but cannot fall.

# Carleen Hicks

The first live person I saw was Mike Piggins. He came up the walk with his leg bloody and the skin hanging off. Like a dog had chewed him and he'd struggled to get his flesh away from the teeth. He was a sorry state coming out of the sunrise and some folks might run from that but I waited for him on the porch like a neighbor does. He stood with his head down, the sweat running off like a fever. The leg bleeding fresh. His breath quick and weasel-thin and him looking at the sidewalk. As if words were written there. Or a puzzle to work out. Finally he fell down on the steps. I put my good arm around him and we sat like that as the dawn turned green under a bank of clouds.

Mike said his whole family was gone up into the sky. He said the wind sucked them out of the crawl space and carried them off. I asked him did he search the property and he said it was gone, the whole thing a blank space by the road. House and tool shed. The fence. The lawnmower and swing set. The earth swept clean like a dirt floor packed hard. Maybe he held to a pipe but he saw inside the storm. All the wood and gravel was in the air. The rakes and shovels and the garden hose. Everything suspended and moving fast. He thought maybe the lawnmower had got him in the confusion, that's what. But I thought maybe farm dogs had set on him just before he got to my place. The mean ones from down the road. I thought dogs. I saw the flesh was torn. The edges of the skin flapping like a scarecrow.

He went quiet for a bit. Things were still spinning in his mind. The blades of the lawnmower over his head, the screwdrivers and pliers clanging as they circled the yard. He said he couldn't hear the screams as his people went flying but their mouths were open. He said they flew away like angels and the cloud opened to take them in. Mike Piggins sat on the step with blood running down his leg and cried. I wanted to ask about the mean dogs, to ask if he saw the shiny things in the bushes, but I didn't. I said a small mercy prayer for his family and watched his mind turn over. Sat with my arm hurting and the day moving on. Then the sunlight went brassy and we both looked at the horizon like there was wind coming.

I want to tell you that we joined forces. That I went back inside and found a sheet to bind up his leg. That we helped each other to safety. But the truth doesn't always happen like you want it to. In the real life, when it wasn't a story to be told, he bled on the porch until he passed out and away. In the real life, I went back inside the house and got a butcher knife. I left his body on the steps and walked carefully out of the yard. Keeping one eye on the azaleas all the time.

# Colonel Stanton

Search teams brought citizens in half dead and clinging to life. We set up mobile hospitals and medics went bed to bed asking for identification. Who are you? Where were you when the storm hit? Lt. Wilcox made a map of casualty patterns. Made a list of names. A bigger list of unknowns. His unit took fingerprints and photos and thought about dental records. Some people we found had been butchered. Some sandpapered. Others had missing limbs. We picked bodies out of piles of rubble. Scraped up the ones that dropped from the sky into vacant lots. The recovery unit talked about flattened armadillos and mannequins and in fact many of the dead were naked like a store window. Angular and broken. Their eyelids gone. That's what Sgt. Mayes reported: eyeballs shining in the searchlights. By 0130 the dead overflowed the city morgue. So we stacked body bags in shipping containers brought in for the purpose. The ones we didn't need in Mississippi. We knew there would be bodies somewhere, though. We always know.

NGOs set up shelters everywhere. Food tables in school cafeterias, cots on the basketball courts, coffee urns in church basements. Rows of tents in soccer fields. The Red Cross handed out blankets and people folded themselves inside. The VFW went block to block with ham sandwiches. It reminded me of the Great Depression, folks waiting in line for a loaf of bread. Or huddled beside the tracks. All those black and white photos. That one mother looking off to the side, her hands chapped and raw, her children in flour sack dresses. Just utter weariness and resignation. And that's what it looked like to me. Like the locusts came in and the fields burned. Like men in fedoras outside the bank. A newsboy on a city street corner selling a headline about Hitler.

The mayor asked people to open their homes to survivors. I wondered about those old FEMA trailers, the ones with the formaldehyde after Hurricane Katrina. I'd seen them below Hattiesburg, parked in a big field like some kind of bad news cotton crop. Pre-positioned and then left behind. Heckuva job, the president said. None of them ever used unless squatters moved in. I thought maybe we would find those trailers some day, scattered around Alabama or Georgia, crushed like Coke cans or floating on a catfish pond. The folks inside or not. The mayor asked but the citizens said no. The citizens were forming up vigilante squads to hunt down looters and rapists. They didn't know yet what they were facing. Neither did we. In those first days we worried about identifying the wounded. Clearing rubble. Moving the body bags into containers. Sgt. Mayes worried about the lidless eyes. Probably he was the only one who had his head on straight.

# Tallulah Ballou

The poet John Keats said negative capability is living in contradiction without reaching for the comforts of reason and logic.

# Everett Davis

It was already dark before I made it back to the office. The power was out everywhere but I saw red and blue rotators, emergency search lights, people with lanterns walking along the road. Ambient light from fires on the horizon. And things gleaming in the bushes. Shining eyes. Feral cats or coyotes slinking along. I heard moans and sighs and sirens. A possum hissing near the dumpster. The sound of bulldozers cranking over. The parking lot looked like nuclear war but the office was completely untouched, not even a window broken. And not a soul was there. Either long gone home or trapped somewhere with clients. Maybe out with a chainsaw or a shotgun.

I searched the office for anything useful. I found power bars, a cake knife, flushable wipes. I found a dead flashlight and some rat poison. Lipstick and powder and hairbrushes. Secret stashes of weed. The light on my phone was bright and sharp and I felt like a burglar. I felt like Watergate shuffling through papers, upending drawers. I don't know what I expected but not the dead man in the conference room. He was covered in blood. His head bashed in. I couldn't tell if he was a casualty of the storm or a victim of murder. How easy it would be, I thought then, to conceal your murder in the chaos of a disaster. Just one more body. One of the wounded who gave up and expired. Didn't make it to the hospital. So sad. So convenient.

I'm not that kind of person, not the kind to take advantage, not a looter in my soul. But I did think about the way bodies become generic in times of trouble, so many piling up that one more makes little difference. Maybe one or two become iconic, the face of tragic death, the child in the arms of the fireman, the dead woman in the wheelchair outside the arena. But scale that to hundreds or thousands and the dead are just a problem in logistics. How to clear them before they rot. Where to put the body bags. What kind of memorial to construct, a wall of names, a hundred bronze chairs, a garden of crape myrtles. Maybe a labyrinth. Maybe a mass grave in the woods.

I sat at my desk in the dark for a long long time.

# FOUR

# Weatherman

When I call for an outbreak I mean that storms generate storms. That turbulence infects even a cloudless sky. That a skin of humid air is susceptible to penetration by viral cells. When I say outbreak I mean there will be days and days of weather. One tornado giving way to another. One vortex couplet collapsing only to reorganize in the next county. And you will be caught off guard. The wind will fall silent. Damage assessment teams will schedule a survey. Sirens and chainsaws will mark the hours. The wind will be still and you will see hours of sunlight, but do not be deceived: the sun is a fever in the heavens. Heat rising off the battered earth, off the cracked concrete and shattered lumber, the heat of massive death and decay, of rotting swamps and blistered trailers, everything warm will rise to converge along a wall of air. So if you have abandoned your safe place, start seeking another. This is not over yet.

Perhaps when I say outbreak you will think of ebola, of people bleeding from the eyes, their organs liquefied inside the skin. You will wonder about the quarantine, yellow flags flapping outside contaminated homes, hazmat-suited medics roaming the streets. You will think of the isobar on the weather map as a boundary that cannot be crossed. And you will worry about the military force that now guards the rubble. The helmets. The weapons. Is it live ammunition, you will ask, and will they shoot to kill if I run? As if you could run from such a storm, this system that extends across space and time. Weather so massive it requires extinction level planning. When I say outbreak I mean that in an office somewhere on the coast they are drawing red lines on a satellite photo. Here and here, they say, but not there.

If you are older perhaps you will think of polio, of headaches and night sweats, of summertime naps and forbidden swimming pools. Of a cousin trapped inside an iron lung. The terror of confinement. Slack faces and unwilling limbs. Or you will remember a virus on a sugar cube and how you were saved by science. What I need to tell you is this: science cannot save you from the weather. There will be no vaccine. There is only the warning and what you make of it. My voice speaking to you through the night, and the next day, and the day after that. I will not sleep until you have been sufficiently warned. So I tell you now that storms are massing on the horizon. This is an outbreak and you are all inside the quarantine and the guns are pointing at you.

## Lila Jane Smith

The chair holds me like my dad did the day I almost drowned. The day I turned upside down in a plastic inner tube and saw the bottom of the ocean. The creeping starfish. Seaweed floating like mermaid hair. A big conch shell waiting to be found. The whole weight of the sea pressing on my chest and my eyes stinging with salt and precious air coming out of my mouth. I couldn't turn over to the light. I couldn't get free of the scalloped edges of the tube. Then my dad flipped me rightside up and held me like I was dead and maybe I was. Just for that moment suspended between the bright sunlight and dim world of the starfish. A dead child drifting away on the current.

Later we went to Acme Oyster House for lunch and he ordered a dozen chargrilled. Dad has one shell from every dozen oysters he's ever eaten and he keeps them in my mom's rock garden like that poem about Mistress Mary Contrary. On the drowning day the restaurant featured oysters from Square Handkerchief Reef, medium oysters, slick and bearded and fat. My father picked over the shells steaming with hot butter and lemon and wrapped one in a napkin to take home. Then there were clouds over the canal and back at the beach and by sunset the lightning was crossways in the sky, a warning about the weather to come, maybe a hurricane washing over Cuba, maybe a waterspout spinning up offshore. I made a fort with the blankets and thought about starfish, so fleshy and slow, how they die and harden in the air.

Sometimes I feel like I can't breathe up here. Sometimes the chair seems to roll onto something solid, like a floor in the clouds, tiles and metal siding, the entire roof from a farmhouse, maybe a section of pavement sucked up off the road. I want to brake with my feet then, to stop and get off, but you know I can't take that risk. Can't let go and stand up. I see the shiny people shake their heads at me: don't do it, they stare at me, don't step into the cloud. You will fall to earth like sea glass through water, and what about the sharks? what about the things with teeth that lurk in the seaweed, the azaleas of the sky? but even I know that sounds crazy. The dangerous things up here are not fish.

Maybe I cry a little bit when the chair lands on the false floor as if it were normal. As if the dentist appointment was finally over and I could go home. Except I am sure I saw a flurry of oyster shells a while back, a dust devil inside the storm, the shells shining with edges that could cut your skin or scoop out your eye. And I thought to myself: silver bells and cockle shells. Pretty maids all in a row.

## Carleen Hicks

The road west was blocked by a tank. My hand to God, a leftover Iraqi tank standing between me and my daughter in Mississippi. So I turned toward town where flocks of crows wheeled up into the sunrise. The mist off the cotton fields met the light out east and the air was green and swimmy and very very still. I walked real careful like the road might break under me. I didn't want the shiny things in the bushes to hear me. I didn't want the tank to notice me walking away.

When I was a girl a man came around twice a year to sharpen the knives and scissors. My mother always hid me in the back room but I could hear the clatter of the blades as she placed them in a basket. He set up his tools on the porch and worked all morning while I sewed buttons on a piece of flannel. In my room hearing the whine of the sharpener and my mother's low voice. In my room thinking about edges and how the porch would be cool and shady and maybe they had lemonade out there. The clink of ice cubes and the way the sweat runs down the glass. The hot flannel and the needle's open eye and sometimes a nap in the swelter of the room. I had a big collection of buttons in a metal lunchbox before the storm hit and I hated every one of them. Now they are scattered to the wind and the crows will think they are seeds.

A broken arm hurts more than you think but also less. Too much to bear the weight of a shotgun, but you can tuck your butcher knife in the sling and carry on. Slowly and maybe with a little fever in your arm, but functional. So I walked the road and pretty soon the farm dogs were sulking along behind me. Sometimes one would bark and the others would snap at it and there'd be a scuffle. Then silence. The yellow lab carrying a toy in his mouth. The hounds nosing the air. All of them watchful and sullen and fearful. Their eyes on me like I meant something to them.

Me and the dogs kept on as the clouds got thicker on the horizon and the air fell heavy and a wind started to rise. We saw the dead people along the way. Some broken and twisted by the storm. Some standing upright and naked and just barely still. Like about to move if you looked away. Like that show my daughter loves, with the time man and the terrifying angel statues. You can't look away or the angels loom up at you with screaming faces. So I kept my eyes on them as I passed and the dogs growled and whimpered. I kept my eyes on the bodies and my hand on the butcher knife and thought about my daughter and how she always wanted to travel in time.

# Colonel Stanton

We tied the wounded to their cots to keep them from breaking their own bones.

# Tallulah Ballou

The poet John Keats said negative capability is living in contradiction without reaching for the comfort of reason and logic. To be able to hold opposing realities in the head, to move forward without forcing a resolution of that tension. And I thought I understood what that meant. Then I saw a pile of plastic bodies unfold itself and walk away. Naked and shining in the brassy light of afternoon. Barefoot and silent and eyes wide open. I tell you my brain literally recoiled. The ground rocked under me. I fell to my knees on the concrete of a Krispy Kreme parking lot. I fell down and stayed down.

Maybe I was in a fetal position for a while. The concrete smelled like rain on the way. The concrete was glazed with melted sugar or a sheen of oil or the glare of crushed glass. The Krispy Kreme itself wasn't there anymore. I saw eyes glittering in the dark spaces of the rubble, something feeding on sprinkles, something tracking through spilled batter and flour, rat or cat, something hungry. Once at the county fair I had a homemade doughnut, a hot cake powdered with cinnamon and sugar and it was the best thing I ever ate in my life. The night spangled with neon, the squealing pigs from the barns, goldfish in clear bags. A night to be in love for the first time. Though I was not in love and knew I might never be. So a cold undercurrent, like walking past the merry-go-round and a breeze around the ankles. What lives under there?

Earlier I saw a squad of guardsmen pour gasoline under hedge and set it alight. The branches flashed and writhed as I passed. Earlier I saw a fish tank full of pomegranates or maybe those were hearts, it's hard to know. The light was uncertain, flickers of leaves and shadows and things glinting or fading, my eyes were full of tears from the smoke. I admit that I was lost. I was lost until I saw the Krispy Kreme. The day it opened there was a line so long it took two hours to get a doughnut. No one cared. They loved that sugar glaze. That neon sign: hot now. How I would love a cup of coffee, I thought.

The concrete felt warm under my body. I always wanted a cat named Dinah. I always wanted to see the lobsters dance. The concrete was warm and the air was metallic. I thought the weather was half in love with easeful death. A direct line between the nightingale and the snark. Someone painting the azaleas. I heard thunder in the distance or maybe bulldozers. Maybe I hit my head on something. It was a long time before I stood up. When I had my balance again I walked across the parking lot. I passed the place where the pile of bodies had been. They unfolded themselves and marched away. Nothing but a pack or cards, I told myself. They were nothing but a pack of cards and the day was turning windy and somewhere there was a cat named Dinah waiting for me.

## Everett Davis

I left the office with a TaylorMade putter and six power bars. The streets were full of troops moving equipment and reinforcing tie-downs on medical tents. A forklift loading ammo boxes or maybe caskets. I walked north toward the river as if the river was a rational place to go. I heard sirens, Cold War civil defense warnings, police sirens and train whistles and car alarms. I heard screams in the high school like a basketball game gone bad. A rumble stomping the bleachers. A big ugly crowd, energy thrumming and swelling the walls. Two blocks away the post office was barricaded with dumpsters and armed men standing shotgun at the door. The fish market slippery with scales and blood, fish entrails, overturned baskets of oysters and squid. Feral cats hissing in the doorway. My mother was home alone with her nasty Siamese so I checked the phone for a signal. There was nothing.

I was thinking about redevelopment when I saw them. Thinking plats and permits and what kinds of zoning changes would be in place, FEMA money, how a person might make opportunities out of vacant lots. Thinking new buildings going up and maybe exclusive sales contracts, a brokerage of my own. Big apartment complexes of course. A new doughnut and coffee place, new schools and parks, everything rising up off the scoured ground. Then I turned the corner and there was a stack of arms and legs and torsos on the sidewalk. I thought the teen boutique had emptied out their stock of window Barbies and they were so pink and smooth I couldn't help it. I reached back with the golf club ready to break loose. And dear lord one of them moved. An arm reached out and next thing the whole body was squirming out of the pile.

In my mind now I see the putter shining, arcing up and down, I hear a sound like a plate breaking. Fragments of pink ceramic or brittle flesh or just bones, the air full of grit and glitter, that body opening up and the sinews all dry and twisted. I remember back in high school how the fist would break a jawbone or the flesh and turn it pulpy, how a beat-down brought the body low, the slickness of blood on the hand, but here there was no blood and in the end I couldn't tell between the Barbie and the sidewalk. Just a bit of sand to sweep into the gutter. And then more of them started to move, to shift the pile and untangle the legs and arms and I ran like hell. I ran until I couldn't breathe and I know I saw other piles and stacks of pink bodies on other corners, in parking lots, one walking in the middle of a street, but I ran like hell to the river. I didn't jump in. I just stood on the riverbank and looked at the water, the sirens screaming behind me.

## Juan Reyes

I heard the sirens again as I neared the shelter and *el gato muerto* put its claws in my neck and I felt it but did not feel it because the claws were dead but it hissed at the soldiers at the door and they did not see me. Their eyes were a thousand miles away. I did not speak to them but went inside as if I belonged and so many rows of cots. Blankets folded or tossed aside. Long tables with stacks of napkins and paper cups. Folding chairs and recycling baskets. The wooden floor of the gymnasium sticky with spilled juice. A puppet show strangled in its own strings.

I called out to *mi mujer* but no answer. I circled the floor searching for unlocked doors, hiding places, storage bins. Where they could put people. Especially the children, the children will fit in small spaces. Like *los gatos*, they will hide when they are hurt and frightened. Inside a cardboard box. Under a pile of laundry, wrapped up in warm towels, *gatitos*. But when I called out the walls echoed and no one answered. The air trembled with emptiness, it rippled with silence, and all the blankets and paper cups and nothing on the paper plates. No radios with music and no jigsaw puzzles, only the puppets with angry faces. When I went out the soldiers did not speak to me.

Beyond the shelter the wind was rising and such clouds like the mountains had come down from the sky. I stood in the middle of the street and was alone with the sound, the cat cradled in my arms like an infant and there was lightning above the ruins and when I stroked the dead cat sparks crackled under my palm. I did not know where other shelters might be and when I asked a man stacking bodies he looked through me, his gaze on the mountains, and I saw what he saw, all the granite of the heavens bearing down. The peaks of Jemez or Cimarron on a summer afternoon turned black with hail and flash floods and a brush fire started along the roadside or the whole of the mountain sliding sideways. That is what he saw but he didn't know it yet. He didn't know the sky and earth had changed places in his heart.

I turned toward where the hospital was or used to be.

## Vesuvia Morris

I spent that first night in a vacant house. A white bungalow with a broken back, a giant oak tree in the bedroom, the kitchen pristine and fussy. Porcelain swans on the piano. There was a crocheted cotton throw on the couch and I wrapped up in that and rested under the dining room table. Wanting something solid over my head while that oak ticked and settled. Thinking what lived in the branches, maybe tree roaches the size of dates, that crusty brown madder with notes of purple lake. The sound of sirens and gunshots and screams filtering through the leaves.

If I slept I dreamed of art class, the nude model wrapped in a paisley robe that slipped from her shoulders, the teacher's black Newfoundland asleep on the wooden floor. The scritch scritch of charcoal on drawing paper, the scent of coffee from an urn near the window and the north light and that boy's yellow fingers from unfiltered Camels. The sound of paper flipping over, a clean sheet, the model taking a break. Someone scraping a pencil with a penknife. If I slept the scrabbling sound wasn't a rat or a host of roaches and the body was something to be sketched, and not something I found broken in the bathtub.

The morning was viridian, I thought. And a patina over the sky, as if something in the air had substance and had aged. The early shadows flattening as the clouds covered the sunrise. Then something coppery in the humidity, a streak of ultramarine in the wind. I walked with my head down against the light, trying not to see the dead, hoping the azaleas were not blooming. Or the awful watermelon crape myrtles. I walked with bruises in my eyes and my flesh nauseated and chilled. Thinking maybe the weather is a palette of things we cannot quite see. The way the blind feel colors as heat, sandpaper, silk. Maybe like that.

# FIVE

# Weatherman

When I tell you the storms are training I mean they are moving like a freight train of identical shipping containers. One cell following in the track of another, holding close to the shear boundary. Heavy clouds scraping along a river valley. A supercell caught by the piedmont fall line or a depression in a soybean field. A corridor of flash winds, one tornado sweeping up after another, the land scoured down to bedrock. The 4:20 from the Norfolk Southern, metal containers stacked and tagged with graffiti, the tracks underneath shining and parallel. Can you see the wheels, relentless in forward momentum? Spinning like the disc of dust where the funnel meets the earth?

These storms are training and there are just days or hours before the next cell arrives. Think of the gap between storms as narrow and vibrating, like the air between the train cars, a mirage of heat and sound. A space that flickers like an old film, things on the other side of the tracks just visible, another set of witnesses, someone seeing you seeing them, but only in increments of light. Like the lines of the rails, you will never meet, a mathematical constraint as serious as the barometer, as true as rain.

I tell you this outbreak is training. That you sit at a crossing counting boxcars and the noise of steel on steel rattles your windows. And now you notice that the tankers are coded and marked with hazard warnings. And you see places where toxins have dripped and eaten into the metal. Pale faces gaze out from the cattle cars and you see those too. The train whistle dopplers and the gravel of the roadbed shifts. The red lights flash like a close encounter. You check to see if you are in park. The barriers are down and the boxcars keep coming so you count them. You count them the way we count storms.

# Tallulah Ballou

When the second storm hit it might have been after noon or almost sunset. It was impossible to track the time and the metallic light had turned fizzy, like steel dipped in acid and fulminating. I left the disappeared Krispy Kreme with wind rising and warming, wet against the cheek as if I had been crying and probably I had. When I looked up I saw the ashes of fireworks falling, the after-image of a grand chrysanthemum, my eyes deceiving me or else ribbons of darkness trailing down to the ground. It made me want to look for rabid dogs. It made me want a scarf over my hair and a cross around my neck.

The streets were nearly empty. Some troops here and there. A truck in the distance. A family of four sheltered under a clear plastic tarp as they shuffled across a viaduct in lock-step. Airborne Toxic Event, I thought: I am living in a postmodern novel and all the disasters we simulated have come true and still we are not prepared. I held out a palm to check for spackles of chemicals, for the small pellets of a virus, but nothing. Just the damp air, almost solid, oxygen in gel form, so thick I could hardly breathe. I thought I saw a child wander into a schoolyard but when I followed there was only a chain link fence, a privet hedge, an overturned yellow bus in a vacant lot. The school a pile of rubble and some of it smoking. That peculiar yellow and what would be inside that bus? I am ashamed to say I kept walking. I didn't look.

Part of the day was gone, I know that. I thought I saw a man but I was wrong. I thought I knew where I was but I was wrong about that too. I do know the sky hardened before nightfall. That sirens sounded and a small tornado dropped down, as if targeted, and worked its way through the rubble. And then three more of them, moving in a pack, the sound thinner than before, a dentist's drill, a mechanical whine. It hurt to hear it and I sensed there was more sound, just outside the range of what a human ear could stand. And I ran. Of course I ran and I thought I heard others running but that was hail hitting the concrete. I took shelter in a culvert with the rats and possums and other frightened things. And I thought how at the end of the novel everyone thinks there's been an apocalypse but things are just the same. Except the grocery store has been re-arranged. Things are not where they used to be.

# Colonel Stanton

We tied the wounded to their cots to keep them from breaking their own bones. A fever twisted their arms and legs into knots and they howled with pain and thrashed the blankets and rocked from side to side. I saw small bones shattering through skin. Bruises purple and yellow like the sky outside. A second line of storms had gathered and the lights flickered and rain started to fall. The sound of the rain on the canvas was like being inside a drum. A relentless pulse and vibration. And the wounded moaning, even the nurses unsettled, the fear of death a thickness in the room, everyone writhing and reeling. Some of the near-dead stiffened and struggled to rise and walk. Medics tied them down and iced their throats but we didn't have much hope for them. We had body bags stacked and ready to go.

Sgt. Mayes reported citizens vanishing from the shelters. Just gone and the aid workers with them. Steam tables and sleeping bags, pallets of bottled water, mops and buckets. Maybe a Barbie castle or game of Monopoly or a tray full of juice boxes. Some baby socks on the wooden floor of a gymnasium and that was it. Mayes said maybe they went to Mississippi but that wasn't funny and I sent him down the line to do a shelter count. Take a squad, I said, and get me a read on operations. Update the rosters. He said everyone was clearing up those pink things and reinforcing the tents and moving equipment ahead of the next storm. Said a count of the living could wait but I didn't agree. I thought then that nothing would be more important than accounting for lives.

I wanted to explain about probability waves. How potential exists in suspension until something collapses it into reality. Like Schrödinger's cat, waiting for an electron to trigger the poison or not. The cat is both dead and alive, equal probability, until you open the box and look. And then you know. The probability crested like a wave at the beach, and then fell, and the cat is dead. Or alive. So I wanted Mayes to open the cat box, to see if people were dead or alive and where they were and in what condition. Maybe we needed eyes on them to keep them whole and in place. Otherwise something would crest inside them and a fever would rise or they would drift away, leaving faint traces, a doll or a sock, an index of presence, a sign of loss. The track in a cloud chamber, a particle passing through condensation. Something too small to be lifted by the wind. But important. I felt it was important.

# Lila Jane Smith

I hear birds sometimes and I think their wings are torn by the wind. That rising notation like from roadside birds, the song they make in the wheels of a car. Or maybe like cicadas, a terrible shrill across the sky and in the darkness of the leaves, dusk falling and the bats and the stars, everything coming out sharp. But up here a kind of scream and then feathers and bone in the air. The wings falling to the ground far below as if a war of angels. As if fragile bodies could not survive in such a storm.

I do not feel protected in this chair. I am sure that things have penetrated my skin, that my flesh has opened and peeled back. But I can't see that, and if my limbs have fallen to earth I cannot tell. I think I am still holding on to the arms of the chair. That the little wheels are turning like a carnival, that flocks of birds are spinning past me like monkeys, that none of the shiny things are angels, that the earth I see below me isn't the earth I left behind.

I remember that painting at the folk art festival, a spiral of crows, a tornado of feathers over a cornfield. Me holding a bowl of gumbo and rice and feeling a chill down my back. Those crows like Hitchcock. A murder of crows. The painting cost a fortune so I couldn't, but I wanted to take it with me. The yellow sky around the black birds, everything wrong with the perspective. Something you could only see from above, from inside the sky. I bought a blank book instead and meant to keep a journal. But I never wrote a thing on that thick paper. It wanted a quill pen, I thought. It was too important for ordinary writing.

Ever since the dentist I feel like a bird stunned by a clear window. Paralyzed by impact. Silent and still and the cat just rounding the corner. The ground so hard. What does the bird think in that moment when it hits the glass? How do I hold this in my head, that the air is solid and not solid, that the ground is under me but also so far below it looks like a painting. How does birdsong rise from the wheels of a dentist's chair? I know I hear something, a pattern in the click and whistle, a way of rolling across the sky that makes a series of sounds. Arpeggios in octaves of birds. A lesson in scales. I don't want to say chittering, but also that. Until the notes are torn away like feathers.

I am tired of this chair. I am tired of the wind. I want to sleep like a stunned bird in the shade of an azalea. To curl my little feet under me, my wings tucked, my neck unbroken. To believe that the warmth I feel is the movement of the sun across the yard and not the breath of the cat. And even the grass standing quiet. I want the silence of no weather at all.

# Everett Davis

Killing the soldier was a lot like breaking up the store Barbie.

# Vesuvia Morris

Everywhere I walked the wind made shadows across the asphalt, things overhead blocking the light, debris suspended in air so high the sky seemed clear. The shadows skittering like lizards in Mexico, a movement on an adobe wall so quick it caught my breath. The piles of concrete and rebar suddenly like pyramids that needed feathers and skulls to make them complete. A place of sacrifice to the sun or moon and a language lost to time. Jaguars creeping out of the rock with blunted faces so fierce I wanted to kneel in terror.

In such a landscape Frida wore a crown of flowers and painted her body into the earth. Her gaze brittle with polio, so stringent, all eyebrows and flaming heart. A stunning darkness around her always. I remember a trip to Mazatlán, a porch lined with red pots, avocado seedlings or small hibiscus or maybe a spiky cactus. The depth of the shade under the roof, anyone could have stood there unseen. Soldiers on the corner with rifles slung across their shoulders. The sky postcard blue. That day the wind was still and I could hear voices from the *malecón* and I thought they spoke of revolution. Or the Day of the Dead.

But when I saw the lizards I thought: Frida's colors are too strong for this country. Here the light is like watered silk, like an abandoned fruit stand strangled by kudzu vines. You might think of it as coastal, the horizon blurred by gulfstream air as it heads north. But to me it seemed an exhalation from the earth, the light rising like a fog from fields of cotton and soybeans, the shallow catfish ponds, the backyards where flowerbeds conceal small graves. I wanted to paint the light of that day like a miasma, like polio drifting through the city, tendrils of clouds almost at ground level, the light something you could breathe in and it would make you die.

So as I walked something flashed across the asphalt just before the sky closed and went solid again. I thought it was a shadow. And it made me think of Mexico, instead of telling me that I needed to save my life.

# Carleen Hicks

When I got to the edge of town the dogs moved up close, bumping the back of my knees and brushing against my calves. The yellow lab paced beside me, still with the squeak toy but a serious look in his eyes. I could feel wind coming and the air smelled like vinegar and boiled eggs, a cool thread of swamp gas snaking through the humidity. Behind me, where the tank was, I knew the clouds would be thickening. Back west, in Mississippi or all the way to Texas, is where the storms come from.

I admit the arm was paining me and I could feel my own breath was hot. So when I saw the crockery in the gutter it could have been a fever dream. I used to have a big mixing bowl, what I made biscuits in or dipped the chicken parts into buttermilk and stirred cake batter that my daughter licked from the spoon. But back when I had the carpal tunnel I dropped that bowl and it broke into chunks and sharp little shards and some of it became dust that went under the refrigerator. And that's what I thought I saw beside the road. Broken crockery, all of it peachy-pink and some of it glittering in swirls as if rainwater had made eddies. The street full of shards, home store stock, brands I couldn't think of. Peachy peachy pink. And I swear it swelled and shifted as I walked by. The dogs didn't like it. The yellow lab growled low and squeezed the toy hard and the others whined like fireworks was coming. I had the butcher knife in my hand, I can tell you.

I thought I would find the police somewhere but the streets were empty except for the broken bowls. The dogs got scared by dead power lines and a few of them peeled off and headed who knows where. Maybe looking for something to eat but I didn't hold much hope for that. The smell of rotten food was strong in town and probably some of that was bodies, and if the dogs were hungry enough. My arm was so hot. My skin felt hard and I could see muscles spasming and bruises rising up. I wanted water but where were the aid stations? I saw empty jeeps and troop carriers and tents flapping, I saw a police car smoking and golf clubs scattered in the road. I thought I saw something chewing on a body and it wasn't a dog. It wasn't a dog, I'm sure of that, and I had the knife in my hand but I was running the opposite way, and overhead the clouds. Overhead a purple kind of thunder and I saw lightning strike the street and the asphalt opened up and lava underneath.

The yellow lab said we should go toward the river and maybe he was right. But I wasn't taking orders from a damned dog so we headed for the center of town. The government buildings would have something to drink and maps of where the shelters were. I was thinking about infrastructure, the things that hold a city together, and who knew there was lava under this town? Who knows that kind of thing? The government.

# Juan Reyes

*Mi abuela* had cancer at the hospital that is no longer there. I sat with her in the walled garden where the women who will die have sun and roses, a little fountain like a creek where *las truchas* are quartz pebbles, such deep blue the veins on her hands and the sky overhead and *el gato muerto* making noises like gas escaping from a pipe. Her cancer room painted oyster by my own crew so long ago, the rooms empty then and now the hospital was a paradise of death, bodies covered in white linens, the big windows curtained in purple like the edges of mountains, the garden full of rose petals and snow drifts from the broken crape myrtles.

In summer the cottonwoods did that, sent dandelion drifts of white against the windshield. The high leaves flashing like metal in the sky. A clanging like bullets against a road sign. In the *arroyos* the National Guard dusting prairie dog burrows, a black plague on their backs, cotton fluff blowing past and a quarantine around the town. *Los perros de la pradera* watching for hawks, the poison yellow at the edge of the burrow, and I thought the hospital was bound by such a plague, the infection carried by the wind, and here were the bodies and all the doctors gone.

I looked at the faces of the dead. I lifted sheet after sheet, my fingers almost transparent with grief, and so many who died in fear, who saw the wind and took the gravel in their eyes, their hearts cracking open, so many who died pierced by the bones of their own homes. I lifted a hundred sheets off faces I didn't know and then on the third floor *mi hermano* called my name and I dropped the cat and ran to him but he was dead the diamonds on his face from a chain link fence and he spoke to me of a paint brush inside his brain. The bristles back and forth leaving tracks.

Making a terrible sound like pine needles falling through very cold air. The cat backing away from his words.

Time passed inside the hospital like inside a cave of salt. Maybe it was an hour or a year it didn't matter because the air was so dry, the hallways so hollow, the air an echo of thunder. I saw the window glass streaked with blood or a hard rain and outside in the garden the sirens. *Mi hermano* said he saw inside the storm and it was full of granite. Also rose petals. And *los muertos, los muertos rosados, los cuerpos*. Did he see them, *mis hijos, mi mujer*, I asked? But he only shook his head and his eyes went white like a blind man. I cried until the oyster walls said I should leave before it was too late and I pulled the sheet over his terrible face and he was dead again. I picked up the cat and walked toward the lightning.

# SIX

# Weatherman

When I tell you the tornado is at the intersection two minutes ago I mean the radar beam circles slowly and we will never close that small gap between past and present. I mean that we live in a world of imperfect information, and the tornado is at the intersection, but two minutes ago. That meteorology is bound by the uncertainty principle. Because we can measure the forward motion of the storm cell or we can witness the funnel as it takes out a transformer. But we cannot tell you where the storm is when you see it on radar, because that moment has already passed.

Look at the hook echo, the classic hook echo, the trace of a tornado that has formed on the southwest flank of a storm. See how the image curls like a fist, like a crescent moon, like the claw of a hammer? How the shape lags behind the rain shield and lingers over a parking lot? You might think of fingernails scraped across a chalkboard or the heels of a dead body dragged through the mud, but you might also think of a crocodile and how it swallows time because that is what a storm does. It moves away from itself on the screen, disrupting the space-time continuum, sucking the life out of gravity as surely as a black hole at the center of a distant galaxy.

Look again at the hook echo. Two minutes ago the hook curled around a hail core that showed hot pink on the screen. The radar caught the hail as it fell from the cloud anvil and rose on the updraft and fell again. But see the image two minutes later. Now the center of the hook is deep purple, almost black, and though I cannot tell you precisely where anything is, that darkness is the sign of debris high in the air. Four minutes ago the radar beam was bouncing off hail, two minutes ago the beam hit wood and metal and dogs and lawn chairs and insulation. But all we have in the present is a polygon that widens to the east.

There is a tornado at the intersection two minutes ago. And what I want to tell you is that the vortex is a manifestation of uncertainty, a resolution of the potential that ripples through the atmosphere. Here a contingent updraft lofting moisture so high that ice forms around each droplet. Here an area of shear so tentative that air currents avoid it until conditions shift and the tornado becomes real. But not in a form we can measure. We live with imperfect information. I already said that.

# Everett Davis

Killing the soldier was a lot like breaking up the store Barbie. The same motion of the golf club, a twist and then slicing through the air until impact. The way the metal shaft looked against the sky and the blood dripping from the head of the club and how I put my back into it, the muscles a long curve of torque and power.

I found him sitting beside the river with his head in his hands. Full camo and kit, his weapon beside him on the ground, just him, the one guy. I heard him moan as he rose to his feet, unsteady in the wind, and he lurched as he moved toward me. The sky was lowering and all the color was gone from the river, it was black and white out there and I've seen the movies. I know what it means when people moan and lurch toward you with milky dead eyes. I could say it was reflexive, to step back and raise the club. And he kept coming so that can only mean one thing, right? a dead man walking, a zombie moaning and hungering. Like in the movies. So I took the club to him. That's what I did.

Or maybe I recognized him. He looked like Tommy Scott from back in high school except he was dead long ago from that beating in the dugout. So maybe a Scott brother all grown up with a grudge that ate his brain and left his eyes empty. That boy from school told to join the army after he burned down a barn and never heard from again. So many in that family and all of them sure I was the one. The dugout wet with piss and blood. A hot day and Camels unfiltered and too much Mountain Dew. Maybe it was about a girl or maybe how much everyone hated each other just for being alive. That kind of day, and this soldier looked like he came out of a bunker or a dugout and his eyes were too white.

In the end he was a pile of bloody rags. Not sparkle dust like the Barbie. More like cornmeal mush or Waffle House hash.

The riverside slippery with gore. What I think is he should have killed me first. He had a weapon and when I came running up to the river screaming, a club in my hand, he should have drawn on me. But I guess the dead don't think that quickly. He just sat there moaning. Then he rose and his eyes were dead and it was a movie we've all seen before. Someone comes back alive who shouldn't and the ones who react, the ones who take out the undead, those are the ones that survive.

# Vesuvia Morris

I waited out the second storm in a Japanese restaurant that was abandoned and open to the wind. The sushi station in back was loud with flies and yellow jackets so I sat near the door. Soaked to the bone. The light made watery shadows as I wrapped up in a tablecloth. The last time I ate there I had a bento box and red bean ice cream after. Hot green tea. There was a Hokusai print on the wall, an ocean wave breaking, a classic. Like an illustration for that story. A coastal village, the houses facing inland toward the mountain, away from boats and nets and work, until a tsunami teaches the people to watch the water, those who survive. But the print was gone and the wall was streaked with soy sauce.

I felt chilled. Like seaweed in the ocean. Like shaved ice and dead fish and sticky rice. I thought: I would paint this scene in calligraphic strokes. My lips black, my skin bronze, the rain a translucent cerulean. The tablecloth simply the watercolor paper showing through. A scene liquid and formal at the same time. The sound of a bell being struck just inside the frame. Vibrations like beetle wings. A boy with a persimmon watching the brush dip into the inkwell. I would paint a misty volcano outside the window.

It rained at my father's funeral, a fine needle rain, a spiteful rain. In the church no one looked at anyone else, no one wailed or fell out, and the velvet seats were hard underneath. Such a slow and deliberate afternoon. A hymn led by a cousin with a port-wine birthmark on her neck. A spill of laminated death cards. The grass in the cemetery bent over and slick: aubergine and sap green, undertones of ochre and umber. The blades and pebbles. My shoes. The pick pick pick of the rain hitting the funeral tent. An overpowering scent of gardenias. In the distance a train passing. My father in a coffin, the clouds solid, all of us dark and unforgiving. When we got the road mercies we left in separate cars.

I was chilled and wet. Outside the restaurant the rain hammered the parking lot and a woman ran past screaming. I couldn't see what followed her. A momentary darkening of the doorway, a low thick shape. Something denser than rain or wind. I pulled the tablecloth over my head. I pulled the tablecloth over and it was warm just a bit warmer and I couldn't see the door and the rain softened and then all I heard was wings. And it occurred to me that it was early for yellow jackets.

# Colonel Stanton

Mayes never came back. I will say that again: Mayes never came back and all that was left of him was a clipboard of names. Nothing else to show he'd ever existed. He went to check the shelters and maybe got swept up by a random funnel cloud or fell into a culvert and drowned or someone shot him from inside a food mart. A sniper or a feral dog or something pink and shining in the rain. I didn't know what I would tell his people.

The medics moved down the rows of cots offering cups of tea and ham sandwiches, checking bandages, pulling blankets over faces. I sat at a folding table and counted the things we'd lost track of: soldiers, equipment, citizens, the state of Mississippi, the time. Wind billowed the sides of the tent and lifted the roof like a beach umbrella. How they flap and threaten and then finally cartwheel down the beach and people running after them with beers in their hands. And get dragged back or left broken in the surf and somehow everyone was already sunburned anyway. The waves pounding on the sand.

The corporal brought me a report from the perimeter. The barriers, the tanks, nobody in or out unless brought by the wind. She said she was alone out there, her patrol scattered in response to fires or gunshots. She said the perimeter needed reinforcements to maintain control, they asked for more water and ammunition, and more bodies. She said something had followed her for the last half-mile and she kept tripping over boxes of petunias. She was soaked and hungry and as pale as a live person has ever been.

I wiped my face over and over. Rain seeped in through ventilation slits. The canvas steamed with mist and smelled like old socks. A cot flipped over as one of the wounded struggled to rise. Soldiers swarmed around the body and I heard moans and something metal clattering against a cart and then the cot was upright and empty and linens folded like a sanitarium. Some old movie, the hospital beds orderly and the walls white. Thin sunshine and a nurse bearing a tray. Like that, but not, because the body bag on the floor looked like tar, the black plastic wet with condensation. And the men carried it out to a truck that was already full of wet black bags.

# Juan Reyes

*El gato muerto hizo chispas hizo un rayo rosado.*

# Carleen Hicks

The courthouse looked like a comic book, all angles and shadows. The yellow lab saw right away that the government was gone. He circled and curled up in the doorway like a gravestone dog. I walked the hallways making currents in the humid air. All the offices were locked but I heard movement inside. Things rustling and scraping and blocking the light. Upstairs someone had put mannequins in the city court, one at the bench, six in the jury box. A horrible pink lawyer standing to ask questions. Pink lawyer looking at a pink witness. I backed away like a cottonmouth in the grass. Backed away real slow and quiet but with my arm screaming.

The pain was making my skin fall off. The top layer sloughing like a sunburn. The skin underneath rosy and smooth like a newborn but hard and sore to the touch. I thought about taking the knife and cutting off my arm but I didn't feel strong enough to cut through. I wondered about a saw maybe a chainsaw but that might be fever talking. I thought maybe the yellow dog would shake his ears about how a saw tears through muscle and bites the bone and then all that blood. My daughter cut her skin sometimes and she always said it eased the pain of living. I thought maybe she was right but I wasn't brave enough.

I was so thirsty. The kind of thirsty when you wake up from a nap that went on too long and you dreamed a motel that won't stay put and the road buckles and the pines along the road have fire up high even though there's a fog in the ditches and the pavement is wet. And when you see the no vacancy sign it flickers and that scares you. So you wake up jolted and thirsty. Wanting sweet tea with shaved ice. A bottle of plastic water. Where was everybody who was supposed to bring water and sandwiches and first aid? An aspirin would be welcome or even a cool rag a pale hand against my forehead my mother leaning over to see if I was awake. Or just that bottle of water. It occurred to me the newspaper might know.

The street was hot with lava and three blocks of rain to the paper office. I stood on the marble steps of the courthouse hearing nothing but sirens in the distance. I could see the wind but it made no sound no sound at all. The dog rose and stood by me and I thought of us in comic terms, a woman and a dog framed by the doors of justice. The woman's arm in a shirt sling and a butcher knife and her skin coming off in strips. The dog bright yellow with big fangs. Something in the darkness behind them, a flash of hot pink. I would need my daughter to write the caption but I knew it would be heroic and grim. It would be like a headline for the future.

# Tallulah Ballou

I left the culvert just before a flood of garbage and dead rats washed through. I know I smelled like sour milk or concrete before it sets and in a movie I would be running down a sewer tunnel lit by bare bulbs in wire cages. A hand-held camera and the sound of claws. But this culvert was only twenty feet wide and I climbed out into the rain and the dusk was around me like thunder in a valley. Settling heavy and dense and resonant. Sheets of lightning like a theater scrim with scenes in strobe motion, an Indonesian puppet show, I think *wayang, wayang* they call it, and wasn't it something in *The Year of Living Dangerously*? The shadow puppets, a shadow war?

When I came out of the culvert the shadows on the pavement, shimmering in puddles, edging out of the ditch like weasels. The shadows on the broken wall of the furniture store a block later. Shadows under the dumpsters. Getting darker every second and in the distance the backlit funnel clouds still spinning. I listened for the sound of plastic scuttling, a snick snick slide, anything tracking behind me, but only heard the rain and more rain and small debris falling like hail. Then I must have started running because things passed too quickly. I saw doorways flashing past like I was on a train, and I know my ankles were turning and I was gasping for breath and the weasels were slick with the rain. Maybe not weasels. Maybe something larger and growling or slithering or scouring up bits of sidewalk.

A town can be darker than you can imagine. When I finally fell it was full night and the shadows were thick on the ground. The shadows smelled of acetone they were laminated and ropy and the air was metallic with sparks and I thought all my bones were broken. I thought my head was broken. And when I looked up into the lightning I saw them all around me. The weasels were gone and the rain stopped and I felt one touch me. Do you know how latex goes brittle and begins to flake? Or an old cake spatula begins to fracture? Or how a puppet, an Indonesian shadow puppet, bends its awkward body to lift you into its arms? And by then I was a shadow of myself. Scarcely breathing in the darkest town imaginable.

## Lila Jane Smith

I see fireworks or maybe a ruined florist shop in flames. Bright purple streaks of wisteria and golden chrysanthemums all around me. White summer crape myrtles falling like snow. Explosions of roses, rose petals curling up in the heat, such bitter smoke like a landfill on fire. The glittering patter of ashes, metallic flakes and chunks of chemicals, sparklers in buckets of water, and I wish I had some deviled eggs or a slice of melon. A pork loin from that corner store with the KOOL sign outside. AC making the door sweat and blocks away a public pool that was too dirty for us so we ran through the sprinklers and those were chrysanthemums too, circles of water dropping like petals of glass.

My mother always made fried chicken for the road trip to Missouri. Sliced tomatoes and buttered bread. Cans of Coke or a jug of sweet tea and dark plums and Fig Newtons. The car had to be clean and we had to leave early early and get gas at the Shell station. The roads up here don't have gas stations or they would have exploded by now. But I can see families getting out of cars and looking to the west and pointing. No picnic baskets but slamming doors on fingers and flat tires and maybe one child left on the shoulder as the SUV speeds away. A little pink child or a mauve child or an invisible child of many colors. The sun directly overhead. A tomato sandwich crushed by the tires and the car a mirage wavering on the edge of the world. The child standing still.

The roads up here don't have gas stations but I don't need one for the chair. It runs on weather. It runs on the currents rising from the earth, curves along the clouds like a long slow turn around the foothills, skids through the severing sheets of rain. That's what I think. The chair runs on the storm. I try not to think of what will happen when the sky clears. I try to imagine a straight road with a real car and a cooler full of Cokes. My mother telling my father that he should have turned at Joplin. My mother singing that song about the Whirling Dervish in a high sweet voice. Me thinking I'd like a chicken leg and not one that's plastic but one crisp with perfect breading. And it occurs to me now that the swimming pool was just fine. My auntie didn't want us to be in the water with the black people. And I would blush about that but my skin doesn't work right anymore.

# SEVEN

# Weatherman

When I tell you to hide the dogs and children I mean that lightning will strike the gravel outside the screened porch at your camp house. It will split an oak tree in half and follow a water main into your shower. The computer on your desk will melt like a painted clock. You will check the attic for smoldering quilts. Count and recount the thunder. Ask if the storm is moving away or coming closer. One Mississippi, two Mississippi, three. You will hear your mother whisper under her breath: Mississippi, four.

When I tell you that everything negative has already collected just below the surface, I mean the storm forces energy in two directions. That wind and rain collide and separate so fiercely the earth itself becomes charged, things sink and swale and the ground thrums with anxiety. Then tendrils of intention reach up toward thin purple lines that sketch the edge of space. The heavens shimmer with dark energy, something you cannot quite see. The charged particles are as far apart as they can go and between them an abyss, a deficit so deep the storm cannot imagine restitution. But clouds are demanding and must be paid. A channel opens and the sky burns with the heat of the sun. Lightning just grazes your house. Or it strikes the airplane taking you to Cincinnati.

Maybe you have seen it streak from socket to socket across the bedroom. Maybe that night you put airplane glue on your cousin's pillow and hoped he would die and then the storm came. Maybe there were hot days and distant thunderheads or pink thundersnow or broad sheets of light you couldn't account for but something burned on the other side of town. You walked under trees without seeing them tremble. You carried umbrellas with metal ribs or golf clubs or stood alone in an open parking lot looking at the sky.

I tell you, you are lucky to be alive. That the bolt, when it comes, will be thick and writhing and it will make the air around you explode. And when I tell you to spell the word properly, I mean lightning will ball up and roll down the hallway and though you will see a sublime and terrible light, in fact enlightenment is not what is happening now.

# Colonel Stanton

Everybody inside the tent was dead or alive. We had the dead in bags and the live ones tucked under blankets, too brittle to move or treat. The fever had dried them out and they shattered to the touch. All the little bones in their hands broken and their joints going sideways like crab legs after the feast. Tent flaps sucked in and out with the wind. Medics sobbed into pillows or danced like puppets caught in the lightning. And that pale corporal on her knees in the corner, making stacks of gauze bandages, singing just under her breath. Something about oranges and lemons.

Around noon I took a squad out into the storm and headed for the perimeter. The thunder was like mortar fire. A series of IEDs. Like the rumble of the Trade Center collapsing. It was hard to see through the rain but it looked like troops ranked beyond the barricades and backed by tanks. I think that was a trick of the light, though, an illusion made of rainwater and wind. I would have seen the orders for troop movements. I would have been informed that we were inside, quarantined with the survivors. I would have seen those orders. I am in the chain of command. My orders were to keep people out of the disaster zone and those were my barricades. So I don't think there were tanks. Or troops. Or IEDs.

We took the jeep back the long way and surveyed conditions in the zone. If I had to report I would say we had lost control of the situation. Buildings smoked and hissed or broken windows and looted or piled high with mannequins. Civilians in full camo pointed shotguns at us as we drove past. Packs of dogs dragged squirming bodies down the sidewalk. The first shelter we stopped at was empty and so was the second. Ham sandwiches rotted on long tables and flies swarmed overhead. In the high-school gymnasium we found two dead boys holding hands and rats eating their eyes. Don't ask me what we did about that. The rain. I keep remembering the rain in the gutters. And how the town looked in the afternoon light as the sun got lower behind the clouds. Like some kind of painting in shades of gray and gold, the world after the great war. Everything broken and the gutters full of water.

When we got back to the medical tent everyone was dead. Their mouths stuffed with gauze. The corporal in the corner with a bullet through her head.

# Juan Reyes

The dead cat made sparks he made pink lightning. His fur crackled under my hand and my skin hissed like picking up an iron skillet. I dropped him into the gutter and he exploded like fireworks but he was in my arms all the time. He was there and not there. I could see through his eyes into his skull and it was a geode sparkling, a stone broken open and washed by the creek of time. I knew this was my cat forever, dead or alive, *mi gato milagroso*.

I felt the wind pressing against my back like tires against a road, the day we drove down Red Mountain Pass into Ouray and a storm was at our feet, the lightning sideways across the highway and the tires slipping, the wind pushing against the car. How we drifted down into the clouds inside the lightning and the thunder snapping *los pinos*, the mountain vibrating with iron ore and sorrow. And when we came out of the mist the Uncompaghre River running high and the car full of the heat of our bodies. The lightning far behind and everyone still alive.

A lot of people die on that road and their spirits linger, *los fantasmas del paso*, pressing against the sheer cliffs to hold back the rockfalls. *Mi papi* showed me their tears seeping onto the highway from the broken granite, *pequeños riachuelos de dolor*. So I believed the dead of the storm were all around me as I walked away from the hospital, crowding me on the sidewalk, stroking the cat and making sparks. Their grief rising from the ground like a mist, their tears filling the gutters, the thunder like the sudden silence of their hearts. I felt them only at the edges of vision but *el gato*, he saw them, and he growled or he purred according to his understanding of death.

That drive down the pass ended beyond Ouray, beyond

Montrose, it ended at the Black Canyon and we walked the edge of the canyon in golden sunlight. We spent the night in Montrose, and what I remembered under the pink lightning was the taste of those apricot preserves, forgive me, I was so hungry.

# Carleen Hicks

I walked on the lava like a tiki bar in Hawaii.

## Lila Jane Smith

I close my eyes but even the darkness is bright. Like a total eclipse. The dark center of my retina surrounded by a halo of golden fire. The storm has sucked all the light off the earth and it swirls around me and the pink people shine like fireflies and whatever bumps against my chair gives off sparks. I am cold and hot and my bones show through like an x-ray or I see floaters behind my eyelids like shrouds falling in tatters.

The angels sing to me but the words are so thin they break up into random letters and I have to pick them out of my hair like bits of grass. Like rolling down the hill in first grade, the sky turning over and over and voices tumbling and the grass so sweet. I am dizzy with sunshine and apple juice and there's an angel in the hydrangea bush but when I roll again it's fire ants and that's how this cloud feels. Prickly but full of blossoms and words I can scarcely hear. The chair about to go end over end down a hillside that ends in concrete.

In my head I see the higher ground I'm living on, the fields of petunias and dog roses and rivers full of flying fish, the hills that dissolve into rain. A farmhouse with Jesus in a plexiglass box and a bird bath and a wagon wheel planted with dill for pickles. A cage full of monkeys at a roadside zoo. People walking along the road, their shadows fuchsia in the afternoon light. None of them look up or sideways or wonder how their feet make the land happen. They just walk in a state of grace. Or they walk with fire ants crawling up their legs and their skin cracking under the sun. Or it is as dark as it is behind my eyes and I hear them shuffle through a windless night. Never speaking. Making the land happen.

When I went to Vacation Bible School we made paper

lanterns in rainbow colors and there were picture books with Moses parting the water and making land for the people to walk on. Behind him there were dark clouds rolling up on Pharaoh and in the distance a host of angels watching from inside the sunset. The Israelites scared to walk on the new earth so full of stranded crabs and lobsters. In the wind the sound of singing. O come angel band. That's what I hear when I close my eyes.

# Tallulah Ballou

The puppet hands. They touched me and lifted me and pat pat patted against my face and neck. Like ants tending peony buds, something I read about in an obscure poem. A farmhouse on fire, a fog rising from the river, a cistern full of frogs. And the ants, a thousand tiny touches, grooming the buds until they bloom like drunken roses. Extravagantly. Reckless flowers that toss when the wind rises. The poem waiting for some kind of storm. Metal lawn chairs on the porch. The ants so patient and serious.

I heard the rain tapping on plastic or concrete and nothing growling just a dank breeze and my ankles aching. I might have been inside a gas station or a warehouse, a trace of gasoline in the air. Walls broken by the wind and lighting strobe flashes. So many of them crowded around me I could hardly breathe and tap tap against my skin and sometime a shiver like a jellyfish tendril across my arm or leg, a sting or slice and I couldn't tell if I was bleeding. The air thickened with the smell of Barbie hair and I drowned in a box of latex gloves dusted with cornsilk powder and the jellyfish floated above on gasoline vapors. I must have fainted and hit my head on the concrete floor because I was out for hours or days or the rest of my life.

When I woke up I was alone. My skin was smooth as if buffed with emery cloth and my head was wading through fields of soybeans and cotton. I saw my car at the state line waiting for me to turn back. I felt the culvert close in around me and the weasels all in a row. The broken walls of the warehouse were split into shrouds of gray and I thought morning was coming and mist was rising. There was a drumbeat to the rain, the ants going down into the earth, and somewhere up north, somewhere in Indiana the peonies were in bloom. And I was sitting on metal lawn chairs on a porch with the house on fire behind me.

# Everett Davis

It was easier the second time or the tenth or how many ever there were. I walked along the riverbank and they came out of the bushes or down the path from the library or loomed up out of the mist and everything was a weapon now. The golf club, a rifle butt, the stake from a sign by the road. The dead lurched and fell and the weather closed in and the sound of the rain was like the pounding of flesh, thock thock thock, huge drops like water grenades that exploded when they hit the ground.

I am sure they didn't scream. They turned those dead eyes to me and their mouths opened but it wasn't a scream. It was the wind stripping leaves off the trees or funneled through a chain link fence. It was a zombie moan distorted by the water in the air. A sound effect of the mind. So the golf club and the stake and stepping over the bodies. I walked until they were lit by the fires downtown and their eyes were as red as mine. And if they screamed how could it matter because they were already dead.

I took shelter for the night in a furniture store. The couches near the broken windows were wet but I knew the bed displays would be deep inside the store. The air smelled of smoke and mildew and something else that made me think of Play-Doh, maybe vinegar? I made noise so the undead would come but nothing crawled out of the darkness so I curled up on what looked like a beach cottage display and fell asleep. I dreamed about a tall blonde with a white convertible driving down curving roads and a red scarf around her throat, the road curling up behind her like an ocean wave, and the air full of knives with wings. I pulled up beside her in my real estate car and when she turned toward me her face fell off and there was nothing there but skull. Gleaming teeth without lips and also her hands were bones, she was a skeleton all over and the scarf was a ribbon of blood.

I woke up screaming except I wasn't making noise. It seemed like hours had passed but maybe only minutes and the fires were still making the walls orange. I saw silhouettes of stick people dancing or writhing and then they were all around my bed like a department store, the poses so awkward, but their eyes were shining pink with rain and they had golf clubs raised like lightning rods. And I woke up again and the night was darker because the flames had died down out in the street and the shattered windows let in the rain and wind but I was deep in the store with a star quilt over me.

# Vesuvia Morris

At dawn I slipped into the bowling alley next door. Inside the arcade, mannequins stood in front of pinball games like pink flamingos at a chrome motel. A reek of smoke and aftershave and sweat, buzzers and flippers and electric cords, slots for tokens, long bird legs pale pink in the gloom. The lanes lit by a ceiling that was cracked like poolside concrete. Hard tables and chairs, score tablets, stubs of pencils and broken bottles. The room echoed with clattering debris. I heard a ball slide into the gutter. That heavy roll and rackle, the three holes like a face turning over, a horror show head with marbled skin. I edged behind the counter looking for size eight shoes and thought: when did they stop using human pinsetters?

In the parking lot someone had lined up bodies the way you do rats pulled out of a bucket. One two six and the heads smashed in. Their arms by their sides as if bound in wire. A study in stillness. The dark gray pavement rusted by blood, a silver sky reflected in puddles, the wet clothes of the dead a palette of dull hues. My art teacher once read us a story about the world before the atmosphere made color possible. A bleak and barren landscape of neutrals, and then the awful shock of the spectrum. The world stunned and almost blinded.

To paint that transition. They tried it in Oz and came up with emeralds and poppies. But there's a color deep inside a pearl that doesn't have a name, and maybe that is where I'd start. With a fine sable brush and softly, to keep the canvas from breaking. I stood at the edge of a puddle thinking: blush and chamois and Naples yellow light. A faint tint of manganese blue as the air thickens over the equator. The prism trembling in my hands and then shattering. A strike a strike the lanes are lit by falling glass and what about that gutter ball anyway? I thought maybe a pair of dry shoes but that face turning over and what if the plastic people were not a harkening back but harbingers? The story was postmodern. She told us that and laughed.

# EIGHT

# Weatherman

When I tell you the storm has an eye you will think of tropical cyclones and you will not be wrong. A tornado wraps around a center of sublime stillness, it curls like a cat around a patch of fog, it spirals inward toward a core of silence, a reflexive lens of grace. It holds a point of balance like an egg upon a spoon. And it gazes at you through a haze of heat and moisture and wind before it destroys the world around you.

If the eye passes over your house, do not leave your safe place to investigate the soft tinkling of debris drifting onto the patio, the sudden shaft of bright light that sparks the dust in the basement, the absurd absence of rain. If you are caught outside, do not run to keep up, to stay inside that column of safety. Do not attempt to surf the condensation that approaches like an ocean wave cresting. Instead you must cling to the grass, to the ironwork fence, to the mottled trunk of the crape myrtle, lest your body begin to rise. For here in the still center, the density of air will fail. In the eye of the storm, the weight of the sky will not hold you down.

Think how a hurricane spins and froths the atmosphere, how the air inside the eye thins and fails, how the ocean swells and blisters beneath it. Think of warm currents rising and feeding the storm, how the barometer falls lower and stranger, how the skulls of the unwary expand. And how the storm drives a surge of sorrow before it, how it moves trailing rain bands, how a great tide gathers under the clouds. And what is a tornado but a cyclone of intention, a localized rotation, a dervish that cracks open trailers and gas tanks and pulls windows from their frames?

When I tell you the storm has an eye you will think of Cyclops, the primordial giant who forged the thunderbolts. How his single eye flashed round and fierce. How he roared across the land. How he was blinded with a sharp stick but crushed men under his body when he fell. When I tell you the tornado has an eye I offer this warning: if you open the door and look up, you may see blue sky. But the wall of the funnel moves, and it will break your neck.

# Carleen Hicks

I walked on the lava like a tiki bar in Hawaii. Sweet drinks with pink umbrellas on all the tables. Palm trees out the windows, a silver lagoon with tiny waves. All those torches blazing and the pig coming out of the coals. The yellow dog drooling and shaking. I walked the beach like blocks of hot concrete. I was so thirsty I could drink coconut water. I was so thirsty my mouth crusted over. I walked until my feet melted or I fell into a tar pit. I walked under carnivorous vines that hissed as I passed.

The smoke from the newspaper office made the air sting like acid. My throat strangled. I thought about pineapple juice. The beads of moisture on a banana leaf. A tropical waterfall or the ocean at the center of the earth. Such a surprise. I had always heard rock, but inside the earth a sky without weather and a shore with golden sand, a reverse Hawaii, no tikis or luaus, just silence. Unless troglodytes and that goose was doomed anyway.

Do you know how loud a building is when it burns? Not just the screams but things that explode or collapse and the air slapped back by the heat? The way plastic smells when the flames reach it. How carpets and chairs sizzle. The curtains and staplers and vats of ink. Rolls and stacks of paper and reference books and letters to the editor. The yellow dog sat beside me and watched all the words crisp up and fly away. The news scattered to the wind. Which was blowing gently and it was almost dawn.

As kids we pretended the schoolyard sand was lava, the sidewalk was lava, anything under the jungle gym was lava and if you stepped in it you died on the spot. Fell down and writhed around and then it was headless horseman or the living dead. I walked on the sidewalk. I walked on scabbled ashes or I fell into the gutter to scoop water into my mouth. I gave the dog a bone pulled from a charred body or I bared my throat and handed him the knife. Maybe I saw my daughter in a bonfire of pink mannequins. Maybe the sun came up and crows spiraled out of a lava field. The center of the earth is hollow with a little ocean inside. Paper umbrellas are flammable. They should not be allowed.

## Colonel Stanton

That satellite image. A space like dark matter, a landscape the camera couldn't capture. How we drove across a wasteland that might have been a state we recognized but when we turned around it was gone. This is not a metaphor for destruction. I mean we crossed the Mississippi River and Alabama was on the east side of that bridge. And everyone in the convoy felt that drop in the stomach, the roller coaster descending too fast for the blood to keep up, and some of us fainted and others cried out. And we all agreed that it was not possible and we would not speak of it and we had work to do behind the storms, so we just drove on.

We did our duty. Coordinated with NGOs and kept communications and sirens alive. Patrolled the broken streets. Unloaded pallets of water and MREs and drew quarantines around the sick and stacked bodies for burning and rescued kittens from drains. We made lists and carried clipboards and flame-throwers and rakes and marked walls with Xs. We distributed our forces according to need. We noted the buildings that could not be salvaged. We had meetings about the future. We watched the radar until it was gone and we waited for reinforcements and we set up medical tents. We set up cots and surgical trays and urns full of coffee and unpacked boxes of sterile gauze.

And when the tents were full of the dead or the plastic, when the town was gutted by fire or picked apart by looters, when the weather turned still for a moment or we just got used to the chaos, I took the last squad of men and we drove back to the bridge. We crossed our own perimeter, the barricades we had set up ourselves and no one shot at us, and the outside looked just like the inside. And then we couldn't say why we had set up these zones of protection. Or containment. Who had given those orders. We passed the tanks and they were empty but they were in fact tanks. And we didn't remember asking for tanks. We took the road west past fields of crows eating the eyes of the dead or fields of high cotton waiting to be picked or land that had been scoured by the wind. We saw a farmhouse and a pack of dogs and we saw shreds of translucent Mylar hanging from the trees and what were those things in the azaleas? We drove west. Sometimes we saw a body fall from the clouds.

When we got to the bridge it was too soon. Fifty miles of Alabama and then Louisiana glimmered like a dream across the muddy water. I thought I saw a barge coming down but it was a raft of the dead all tangled up together. The wind made the bridge sway or the grief made our heads swim and the river itself was tenuous like mist rising. And we sat on the levee and wept like the Bible, alas Babylon that great city, alas alas for the magnolias and the pines and the slave cemeteries and swamps everything fading from our memories already and alas for that Rowan Oak place and the man who lived there and wrote books. We sat on the levee in the rain and the wind. And the sign on the bridge said: River.

# Juan Reyes

I left a note on the mantel: *queridos míos*, wait for me at the Ghost Ranch. In my head the low hills, the little goats in the *arroyos*, *los cabritos*, a river of clear flame. Such cool dry air inside the adobe walls the cottonwoods lizards in the creosote bush. I left the note on a mantel a thousand miles away. *Mi casa mi casa*, a house of the dead or missing, how I got back there a tale to be told at the campfire with stars overhead. The terrible streets of a broken town such screaming in the clouds and *el gato muerto* hissing at the azaleas. The soldiers as if struck blind and the curtains billowing in the hospital like plague coming in. The puppets hanging from ceiling fans. How many weasels in refrigerators? How many bodies bloated in the gutter? *Madre de Dios*, the jigsaw puzzles scattered in the hallways. The claws of the cat so sharp.

Say we fried the trout for dinner. Say rice and beans and beer, and mesquite in *la fogata* making sweet smoke. The sparks rising. The sky spangled with fish scales. The beer cold from the river and I tell the pink lightning that splashed the sidewalk like a pale pale blood. I tell the woman torn to pieces by dogs and the magnolia blossoms like pieces of the moon, I say: *mis primos*, you cannot imagine such a state, the mockingbirds and cockroaches, the air too thick to breathe. And I tell how the cars flew up into the storm and I had gravel in my palms. And I say: *Ay Dios mío, la casa estaba vacía*. I say: dear God, the house was empty. Only the cat I brought with me, and it was already dead.

After the storm the house it was empty. I tell that. I tell the kitchen and bedrooms, the shattered windows. And the shelter, empty. I tell a hospital full of spirits, *mi hermano*, *mi abuela*, all the rose petals. And still the house empty even when the thunder fades. I tell that. I tell my heart so cold I shivered. And the campfire it smokes and pops and *mis primos* they ask no questions, they look up at the stars and sigh.

The house was empty. The rooms black with mold. Glass all over the floor. The tomato plants flattened, the habaneros, the pine tree split in half. A swollen rat. Two rats. But the sandbox so clean and level. Forgive me, I could not stay in that place. I left a note on the mantel. I said to *mi familia*, follow me if you can. Take the road west and keep walking. We will meet again at Abiquiu.

# Vesuvia Morris

The quad was sectioned off with police tape. The grass trampled into streaks of cadmium green. At the far edge, the art building all brick and balcony, the despondent robot all rusted ribs and rivets, that skeleton ship filled with river stones. Twists of metal hanging from oak trees, maybe shreds of siding dropped from the clouds. Like found art, or what you frame as you reconsider the world, the rough side of the oyster shell, the terrible beauty of the broken bone.

I took a muddy path around spattered sawhorses, spikes tipped with blood, stacks of empty pallets. A row of dumpsters as the last line of defense or a statement about quarantine. I couldn't look inside because the quad was empty except for the sculptures and oaks and wrought iron benches. The bell tower looming into a gathering mist. I thought cardboard boxes and pizza crusts and what else would go into those bins? Jars of dried paint and clotted brushes, strips of canvas, stained smocks and severed heads. The dumpsters a flat copper sulphate blue trickled in vomit or android blood. Sticky white and mottles of yellow. A suggestion of fingers curling over the edge but maybe just computer cords.

The mist thickened at the edges of the quad and the buildings went ghostly and hollow. A fog or miasma, a density of time. The pathways slick with dew. Then the air brightened as clouds opened overhead and I could see a circle of blue sky. Now the green streaks of grass reflected in the walls of mist and I saw bits of paper suspended like diatoms in water. Shards of glass raining down and pink petunias falling and the blue of the dumpsters shading into swirls of air. My neck ached from looking up at the eye and it felt like drowning. The quad was liquid and twisting around me and I wanted to rise up. I wanted to breathe the blue sky. Then I saw what it must look like from above: the earth a sediment at the bottom of a dreadful pond and all the broken bodies like silver fish catching light.

That first semester in oils we saw a rare black and white film. Claude Monet in a light summer suit, 1915, his white beard jutting as he speaks earnestly to another man, both men wearing straw hats and smoking. Then beside the famous pond, Monet painting *en plein air*, his palette and brushes, umbrellas overhead, and down the garden path a little dog running. What we could not see in the film were the colors, the watered blues and greens, the touches of purple and ochre, the reflections and shadows, the images so delicate and bold. The impression of drowning in light and color and that is what I felt in the quad, that I had painted myself into a canvas. The oils tacky and malleable, the scent of turpentine, the day a bit too bright or hot and so an umbrella and Monet's cigarette dropping ash onto my skin. And what I wondered was: what about the little dog? At the end of the film the artist walks away but the little dog doesn't follow. He takes another path and disappears.

# Lila Jane Smith

Think of a swimming pool. Diamonds of light over the deep blue, a bright yellow blow-up float, the scent of coconut and iodine. I drift with the sun so hot on my skin and dangle a foot over, testing the water. The sun so hot and the water just cool enough or maybe too cold and I test it to see. Then my brother sneaks up under the float and grabs my ankle and I scream. So much splashing and I'm in the water making eddies and my sunglasses sink to the bottom. My father has the grill fired up and watermelon for after supper and maybe thunderstorms later, but right now I see a wasp caught in the water. Wings like transparent leaves and spinning a little in the diamond light.

My chair spins like a wasp around the eye of the storm and when it comes close to the rim I feel the heat coming off the earth. I smell the broken eggs in the grocery stores. The splintered pine and sour insulation, bitter incense or scorched linen, everything rising on the warm air that funnels upward. Gas stations leaking and pond scum thickening, the graveyards sweet like rotten gardenias. A smell of destruction so dense it draws buzzards or shuts down a school or makes people fall out. The kind of smell that stings your eyes.

Then the eye shifts eastward away from me. It's all rain and lightning and the scent of hail as it forms. The petunias frozen in light and gravel pattering and the sound of train whistles dopplering far away. And I see ground under the people who walk through the clouds. Some of them are plowing fields now and looking forward to the future. There are more roads and cars with fins and billboards. A motel with a crescent moon sign. A Waffle House. Rivers filled with mist and catfish. I see pink children in sundresses and magnolias in bloom and I see dirt and pavement that looks solid. So I wonder if there's a choice I could make. To slide down the cliff face of the eyewall and come hard or softly to the stinking earth. Or to walk away from my chair and order steak and eggs and coffee.

I rest on the dentist's chair with a foot dangling in the clouds. I can't feel a solid surface and I slide a little farther off and cling to the arms and stretch my legs into the cool currents of the storm. The deepest pool imaginable. Such dark water all around and shapes moving under the chair as if jellyfish. My legs so pale and pink. I want to get off the chair. I can almost touch the bottom. That Waffle House. I can walk it from here.

# Everett Davis

I clubbed the alligator rats from the sewers and swamps. Rows of teeth smiling inside a drain pipe. The edge of town, rat town, hard and industrial. Wire fences and fuel tanks, the smell of sulfur, pools of water filled with tires and refrigerators. Shreds of insulation floating through the air. A street of body shops and locksmiths and railroad crossings. A sign that said: we buy scorpions.

The warehouse was bleeding rust. The scrap yard was a mess of shredded steel that humped and bulged and steamed. A man came around the corner carrying a chrome bumper and I wondered if the dead kept attachments to things, like the guy just couldn't let go of his car. He lurched and moaned until he tipped over a 50-gallon drum and then the sky skittered and swarmed, scorpions taking wing, a noise like a spoon inside the garbage disposal. How long had he been dead? I had the putter ready for him, but he drifted back toward the piles of junk and I wondered what was in the washers back there, the tubs full of rattlesnakes or whatever.

I knew a man once who kept tarantulas but they turned out to be so tame. He burned them alive one day just to see the legs curl up. Maybe that was me. It's hard to remember now. I did have a dog one time but he got distemper and my dad killed him with the butt end of the hatchet. His name was Morgan. Pretty sure the spiders never got named and also that scorpions don't have wings except here in Alabama. Everything here flies at you like it means it.

Broken buildings made good hiding places. Any number of dead bodies inside the gloom of the FedEx office. I stacked some there and left others where they fell. Whack whack whack-amole, the moans and screams and the sound of the club hitting flesh. Some of the dead begging for mercy. The clouds overhead full of acid rain and the scorpions circling like vultures. I might have been the only survivor dealing with the problem. For all I knew the only one. The world black and white except for the gore. Like a movie. You've seen the movies, right? I had to do it or the world would not be saved.

# Tallulah Ballou

I walked back to the broken library in the soft lull of the morning, the air milky with decayed lightning. The river steaming under a layer of mist. The sound of a motorboat, sputtering like a small Evinrude, someone fishing for bluegill or crappie. I came down the hill into a chaos of insulation and roofing tiles. Crushed cars in the parking lot. A tangle of crape myrtles stripped naked by the wind. I found the little stone lions on the steps gone and the front door sideways. The hallways thick with ash drifted from downtown. I found a restroom blocked by overturned book carts. A spray-painted X in fluorescent orange, the numbers smeared and mysterious.

Or maybe I found the front lawn scarred by bonfires. The stacks filled with skulls. Maybe I slipped in the gore outside the reading nook or found story puppets lined up on the circulation desk. Or heard fists pounding on a conference table or small teeth chattering, the scritch scritch of something gnawing on a computer screen. Maybe the motorboat was a machine gun. Maybe I sat on the steps and remembered screams and sirens and the books sucked out of windows. All those plots scattered to the wind, the pages fluttering like frightened birds, every letter stretched by the absurdity of flight.

After the storm I drove to the state line and turned back. Then doughnuts and weasels and my head against concrete. The smell of gasoline. The rain like vinegar or like a blessing and who could say? The threads of memory are like Faulkner's garden, a knot of bitter herbs and roses. I went to his house in Mississippi once, a square house, white with dark shutters, the rooms so plain and solid. One with a small desk and a black typewriter, another with a novel outlined in pencil on the walls. The scuppernong arbor and the smokehouse, a flat stone labyrinth, a patio overlooking a ravine full of cedar and cypress. I got lost in Faulkner's woods, a path forked the wrong way, and oh the mosquitoes and gnats of that magnolia afternoon. How the time melted there and the earth loamed and sighed and even the air was like honey.

"My mother is a fish" Vardaman says. In that novel the river floods and the mother's body rots in the coffin as it travels the countryside on a mule wagon. Which shows how every plot is subordinate to weather, to summer heat and rain, to the way our bodies respond in the face of barometric pressure. Some of us go mad and burn down the barn. Others use the abortion money to buy false teeth. But none of it happens quite that way if the river doesn't rise. So I sat on the steps of a broken novel. I sat in the ruins and my head swelled with words as if to burst.

# NINE

# Weatherman

When I tell you the radar shows nothing but weather, I mean it in all the senses you can imagine. That solidity is a state of mind. That you were always invisible and the bodies rising through the air are angels. That clouds have motivations and designs beyond your comprehension. I mean there is no end to weather even when the sky is perfectly white. That the Doppler is a plot device, like the polygon, like the torcon number, that everything is about thermodynamics or the expression of differential equations.

Maybe you are waiting for the funnel to rope out, for the wind shear to resolve, for the mesocyclone to dissipate. Blue sky ahead and dry air and a chance to evaluate the damage. But when I tell you this is a Particularly Dangerous Situation, I mean there is no evidence that your town can sustain life. The infrastructure has failed. The river has turned to methane or to blood. Magma has broken through the crust of the earth or the dead have risen or maybe the Mini-Mart has run out of Slim Jims. FEMA has marked the doors and left and now there are strips of Mylar hanging in the trees.

What if the radar could show you this: you are embedded in the atmosphere like a galaxy in the universe. Gravity and dark matter hold you suspended in a web of energy and you travel on the froth of a singular expansion. The air smothers and enfolds you in a dense weave of strings and vibrations. I stand in a windowless room or an elementary school cafeteria or a bunker in Kansas. There is a sheen of sweat on my forehead. A stack of print-outs rests on a table or a coffee cup turns over or maybe an intern says "bubble wrap" but what he means is that you cannot escape the small contingencies of chaos.

Think how the solar wind tumbles the asteroids in space like cosmic pool balls. How turbulence roils the blood in your veins. You are caught in a narrative that might not be survivable. I say this with regret and sincerity and with my white shirt unblemished: the storm has become your universe and there are terrible stars and planets forming in the nebulae of debris. Look at the path of destruction; already the red petunias are blooming there.

# Patti White

Patti White is the author of four collections of poems, *Tackle Box* (2002), *Yellow Jackets* (2007), *Chain Link Fence* (2013), and Pink Motel (2017), all from Anhinga Press. Recent chapbooks include *A is for Aphasia* (2013), *Kontakion* (2014), and *District Flood* (2014). Her poetry has appeared in journals including *Iowa Review*, *North American Review*, *River Styx*, *Nimrod*, *DIAGRAM*, *Forklift Ohio*, *Parcel*, *McNeese Review*, *Slippery Elm, Vine Leaves*, *Waccamaw*, and *New Madrid*; her nonfiction in *Gulf Coast* and *Mulberry Fork Review*. She lives in Tuscaloosa, Alabama.

Made in the USA
Middletown, DE
18 January 2020

83291681R00090